Accounting delivers a lot of [illegible] rarely addresses the business [illegible] standing of the complete financial impact of decisions made as well as decisions to be made. Both functions also have a lot of internal process waste. The Value Add Accountant can provide solutions to all of these issues.

Jean Cunningham and Orest Fiume wrote about their experience as CFO's creating this role in the 2003 seminal Lean Accounting text, *Real Numbers: Accounting for the Lean Organization*. In the years since, Jean has traveled the globe, consulting on Lean process improvement and waste reduction in accounting and other office processes for numerous companies great and small.

This book expands the *Real Numbers* message by providing detailed examples of how to reveal accounting waste, start a personal value add transition, and get buy in on these pivotal accounting changes. This book also describes how accounting can effectively evaluate corporate waste reduction and improvement activities.

You will learn how adopting this new role can enable accounting and finance to proactively support business decision making and impact improved outcomes. This expanded role has both accounting operations and company-wide elements. It is initiated by applying Lean principles and tools to everyday processes to minimize mind-numbing transaction work and other waste from accounting processes. Those improvements increase available accounting capacity. This capacity is then applied to impacting the future with more time spent on internal customer-based, value adding activities for the organization.

Your Value Add Accountant journey starts here.

The
Value Add
Accountant

an indispensable partner supporting strategic
improvement efforts

JEAN E. CUNNINGHAM

 **JCC** *press*

ISBN 9780999380116

CONTENTS

PREFACE

In 1992 I was CFO of a private manufacturing company in Louisville, KY which started adopting the concepts of the Toyota Production System (TPS). I had no idea what TPS was and wondered why anyone in accounting should really care. Not that I ignored it. For I was very curious what this thing was that was percolating through and turning our traditional manufacturing area on its head.

Over the next couple of years, I became a complete devotee, an avid learner and consultant, and, using my CFO position, a fervent promoter of TPS concepts and application for every function. We started using the term "Lean Manufacturing" rather than TPS during this period as well. My view of business had quickly and dramatically changed forever, and I began integrating Lean principles beyond manufacturing and throughout all departments (e.g. accounting, HR, IT, etc.)

In the late 1990's I was asked several times to write about my Lean experiences from the financial professional perspective. I was not an author and really wasn't very interested. TBM

Consulting Group was sure there was a unique, important story to be told, and they finally convinced me when they introduced me to another CFO, Orest Fiume, who had similar experiences adopting Lean and was interested in coauthoring a book. TBM funded our work to write *Real Numbers*. It recounted how each of us worked with our staffs to change the accounting and finance information we distributed to optimally align with the new Lean operational needs in our company. The book won a Shingo Prize for Research.

Later, I became convinced that the story and experience related to changing our information system group processes and output to best support our Lean business practices was worth writing about as well. I convinced Duane Jones, who I worked with in IT, to coauthor the book with me. *Easier, Simpler, Faster* also won a Shingo.

In 2006, I left the corporate world because I felt so strongly that the engagement of finance and accounting to the Lean efforts of organizations was a critical step forward in helping our companies increase their value to customers, to shareholders, and to employees. Since then, I have worked with over 150 client companies and given innumerable speeches and seminars on Lean Accounting as well as other aspects of Lean Business Management.

Today, I remain as convinced as ever, that we in finance and accounting are critical to the Lean journey. And that we as analysts and accountants have to significantly up our game to remain relevant and become high value contributors in the face of the Lean Enterprise transformation taking place throughout the world.

Out of these experiences is the genesis for this book, *The Value Add Accountant*.

The book is not just for accountants. In fact, I apply the term "accounting" with a very broad brush in this book. It is encompassing of accounting, finance, analysis, and all things related to the language of business.

And this book is not just for people already involved with Lean. The opportunity is far too big to just be constrained to influencing one function or one methodology or one strategy. This is about upping our game. This is about making the accounting, the language of business, more valuable to and work better for our companies going forward. We need not be slaves to tradition but can be innovators and value creators along with other functions of the transforming Lean company.

If you can relate to any of the following descriptors, this book is for you.

- CEO and CFO

- Controller, FP&A, cost analyst, accounting manager

- The accounting and finance team members

- Lean Leader focusing on the Lean Office or Lean Business Management

- Accounting educator

- Lean Leader working with the finance organization

- Someone already supporting Lean Accounting

If your role is not listed, but you are frustrated in trying to understand the valuable role that the numbers and the numbers people can and need to play for your company, then this book is for you as well.

The Value Add Accountant builds on the experiences shared

in *Real Numbers*. But, *Real Numbers* is not a prerequisite. Reading both books will give you deeper insights into this topic, but each book stands alone. It is the wonderful ongoing demand for *Real Numbers*—now for over 14 years—that inspired me to add my more recent learnings and experiences to the Lean Accounting body of knowledge. I hope that you will be inspired by these profound changes to accounting's processes and mindset to which I am firmly committed, and that it will become work you also embrace.

This book is not a training guide for Lean principles, tools, or methods though it does reference all those things. So, Lean terms are used throughout either directly, or, when implied but not explicit, noted in parentheses.

If you are unfamiliar with Lean, do some background research for familiarity on any Lean term you come across. Happily, today there is a lot of literature on "What is Lean?" though studying it is not required to read this book. But I hope you will be as inspired as I am by Lean principles and want to learn more.

When James Womack and Daniel Jones wrote *The Machine that Changed the World*, they may not have expected how their writing would so strongly influence sweeping changes in manufacturing. And when they followed up with *Lean Thinking*, they might not have expected that their work would catalyze the expansion of Lean adoption far beyond manufacturing.

And back in 1992, little did I suspect the profound impact to come when we started experimenting with how to get products shipped faster and more reliably to customers using the then curious TPS methodology. Or, that the effort would inspire us to look at all of our business processes in a new way which led to a Lean Office and a Lean Business Management system.

And when Orest and I wrote *Real Numbers*, we had no idea that it would help establish a modified way of accounting, Lean Accounting, to support the needs of the evolving Lean Enterprise.

And now, this book presents additional insights from the past decade on successes in promoting and establishing value for the accounting function, caveats to watch out for and how to overcome them, and methods that I have found particularly valuable to my clients.

I believe this is important knowledge for the accounting professional as Lean principles continue to penetrate companies everywhere.

And, you might choose to be a Value Add Accountant and play a more valuable, proactive role in this accelerating corporate drive for ongoing improvement.

ACKNOWLEDGMENTS

Thank you to each of my clients who have entrusted me to come into their companies and help coach and support them in their Lean transformation efforts over the past decade. Teaching and learning are two sides of the same coin. The breakthroughs, out of the box thinking, and sometimes sheer brilliance I have witnessed while working with my clients makes this work fantastic. We are all enriched.

Thank you to Pat Lancaster, founder of and prior CEO at Lantech, Inc. Pat was the catalyst and enabler for all my Lean learning at Lantech. I would guess many of my coworkers there would concur. Without his trust in all of us, the managers and employees, we would never have been able to so freely and creatively explore how to use those shockingly different Lean principles and methods. Pat empowered without abdicating. He was there with us side by side all the way, contributing as well, but not forcing or second guessing. Thank you, Pat, for the opportunity to experience true leadership.

Last but not least, I give special thanks to my partner of

over 40 years of marriage, Alan Riggs. We collaborate on all the strategy, planning, and scheduling at Jean Cunningham Consulting. Alan is the editor for this book and everything written or designed in my business life from proposals, to presentations, to newsletters. I couldn't do it without him.

INTRODUCTION

Have you overheard these? Accountants as the butt of a joke. Being called "bean counters" or "the corporate police." Never seen outside the ivory tower. Operating at the 5th decimal point. Having no personality. No excitement. Dull. If you are tired of those representations and want to change that paradigm, you are like many others in accounting and finance. But to do so, be aware that you might well have to change your paradigm as well.

In another universe—that would be everywhere outside of accounting—there is a strong desire by non-accountants to understand "the numbers." They know the numbers are necessary and important, but want to know, "What's with the mumble-jumble names? And, why do they often present something seemingly unrelated to the company's products or customers? Why is it so hard for me to connect the dots of the financial statement to the real world I work in?"

Hmmm.

When I enrolled in my Executive MBA program, applicants had to have at least 10 years of management experience. Class members were impressive. One CEO took his company public during the term. Another was buying up nursing homes as quickly as she could. Another sold technology innovations to large tech firms. Another was a medical doctor. Accomplished business leaders all, and two thirds of them said the main reason they were pursuing an MBA was to understand the numbers. As a person with an accounting degree, this was a huge eye opener for me.

Hmmm.

Additionally, research articles in recent years often find CEOs want more business partnering from the CFO[1,2]. American Management Association and others offer courses on Accounting for the Non-Accountant. These are symptoms of a huge gap in the way finance and accounting are approaching the information and decision support needs of the organization.

Hmmm.

This book provides some baseline strategies and tools that we in accounting can use to narrow the large gap between accounting perceived as (and being) an out of touch ivory tower and accounting being a valued business partner who impacts forward-looking decisions and processes and, thereby, helps to improve organizational outcomes.

This gap is sustained by all areas within finance and accounting and everyone from the newly hired clerk to the CFO can help to narrow it in their own way. In turn, the information in this book is not presented as related to a particular job type. Here, "accounting" refers to all those working in any finance or accounting function.

IS LEAN REQUIRED?

The book will frequently reference Lean. Lean refers to the principles, concepts, and tools that were identified by scholars in the late 80's when studying the Toyota Production System and companies that use the concepts. Two books that are the results of these studies are *The Machine that Changed the World*[3] and *Lean Thinking*[4]. They were critical in launching Lean Manufacturing and the Lean Enterprise respectively into the business world consciousness. The company where I learned and practiced these concepts is discussed in Chapter 6 of *Lean Thinking*.

I have been practicing and consulting on Lean for over two decades. I believe in it thoroughly and have consistently seen it work wonders on process improvement. But, from my CFO and consulting experience with many, many finance and accounting teams, I've also seen that the opportunity to improve accounting's usefulness and impact does not rely exclusively on adopting Lean concepts. It relies also on the accounting function's willingness to try new approaches, to experiment, and most importantly to engage with their internal customers.

So, adopting a companywide or function-based Lean strategy—while strongly suggested—is not obligatory to using the techniques and methods in this book. Many can standalone and provide value even when not part of a larger Lean program. I've been told often, "It just makes sense." concerning much of what you are about to read. And, these techniques can help you, but they might well be opposed to how you learned to manage or drive accounting operations.

The title of this book, *The Value Add Accountant*, pulls from the Lean concept of providing value to your customers. And, in this book, "Value Add Accountant" means an accounting professional who is:

- identifying their internal customers,

- interacting with their internal customers, and

- focusing on how to continually increase their value add to the organization.

STRUCTURE AND SEQUENCE OF BOOK

I recommend you read this book front to back. But if you want only to explore specific topics, and so it can easily be used as a future reference book, each chapter is purposely written to stand alone. So, you can cherry pick the chapters in which you have a particular interest.

This subject matter is organized into three sections.

Section 1:
Lean is the best way to drive organizational value creation.
The three chapters in this section, Chapters 1-3, do not describe what Lean is or tell how to use Lean concepts. Instead these chapters describe how to connect accounting with a company's Lean efforts.

Chapter 1, "The Profit Model," discusses a proven way to demonstrate the broad impacts of many improvements to the financial outcomes. It reveals the relationship between value, profit, employees, and Lean activities.

This is a need for most companies, but especially for companies adopting Lean because of the strong focus on taking action for improvement not only in big projects, but in small, unseen-by-most experiments as well. Many non-accountants complain that they do not know how to talk with finance about the value of the waste reduction activities and other changes, and many accountants (and others) think Lean is just about cutting costs. This chapter will help sort out this confusion.

Chapter 2, "Using Trends to Prove ROI," takes on the need to improve communications about the impact of improvement changes. Much of Lean thinking is used to reveal waste in processes, and, then, reduce or eliminate it. This results in many former process actions (e.g. steps, defects, unknown duplication, etc.) no longer occurring and others becoming more efficient. But accounting language and reporting is based on transactions. These transactions only reflect activity that does happen. So, there is often frustration about how to effectively communicate the high value impact of former waste that is no longer happening (e.g. overtime not needed, cost reduction, etc.). This can be a particularly important new role for accounting that will increase its value to the Lean organization. This role can illuminate where change is flowing to the financial results, and also where change may not be having expected impacts.

Chapter 3, "Generating Profit Using Lean," describes the opportunities to convert capacity freed up by waste elimination into resources available for new, higher value activity. In particular, this chapter offers what the accountant needs to be aware of in supporting this capacity utilization and avoiding inadvertent barriers due to traditional reporting and budgeting.

Section 2:
Leveraging Finance and Accounting Information
This section focuses on improvements within the accounting function to increase capacity, improve financial statement usefulness, use financial transactions in new ways, and increase attention on one of the largest but least managed costs, the cost of materials.

Chapter 4, "Close the Books," contains detailed information on how to improve and reduce the lead time of the close process. While every accounting team has a variety of responsibilities, this one process, close the books, is the only accounting process found in absolutely every company.

It is also an important process to focus on as it touches every accounting operation, all reporting, and much of the analysis. It is the "news" that goes to your internal customers, owners, bankers, and auditors. I often find that when an accounting team works together to improve the close, it becomes a gateway to additional collaborative improvement activities.

Chapter 5, "Options for Lean Management Accounting Statements," shows examples of how to align statements with the needs of a Lean company and how to eliminate standard cost.

This is a very important issue for manufacturing companies that are experiencing significant reductions in WIP and finished goods inventory as a result of applying the concepts of one piece (or small batch) flow and pull processing. This is the primary issue that launched the experiments, research, and ultimate establishment of what is now called Lean Accounting and references to a Plain English P&L. It is a significant topic in *Real Numbers*[5].

Standard cost accounting is the root of much confusion when significant reductions in inventory occur. But even without the reduction in inventory, many poor decisions are made using standard cost results. While this book does not address these problems, it does provide alternative presentations of GAAP based statements.

Chapter 6, "Using Defects to Drive Financial Gain," provides a new approach to using all the transactions we see in the accounting data. Instead of just focusing on cost, accounting can take advantage of their unique view of the company by seeing where there are upstream defects and problems in the company processes. Value Add Accountants can work with (instead of against) their operational partners to identify areas where process improvement can relieve stress points in the organization.

Chapter 7, "Materials: Big Cost; Little Attention," is a chapter that will challenge those accountants in companies that have large costs associated with product materials. This area of cost typically gets very little attention, and yet, when delved deeply into, can yield huge benefits in improving company outcomes. Accounting has underutilized data and knowledge that can strongly influence their company's future planning for products and services.

Section 3:
Go Take Action
Chapters 8-10 in this last section, are meant to get you and your accounting co-workers out of your traditional seats and start instigating change. It is indeed important to read what others have to say about the role for accounting in the brave new Lean world, but accounting itself must take action to realize any potential improvements or changes. The chapters in this section, "Get Started," "Communicate Lean Improvements," and "Convince the CEO/CFO to Adopt Lean" provide recommendations on actions to start and sustain movement towards the Value Add Accountant and Lean Accounting.

In the Conclusion, I summarize the Value Add Accountant's role and outlook.

BECOMING A VALUE ADD ACCOUNTANT
The role of accounting is defined in Investopedia in part as "... a professional who performs accounting functions such as audits or financial statement analysis."

An accountant is a practitioner of accounting or accountancy, which is the measurement, disclosure or provision of assurance about financial information that helps managers, investors, tax authorities, and others make decisions about allocating resources.

The Big Four accounting firms are the largest employers of accountants worldwide. However, the large majority of accountants are employed in commerce, industry and the public sector.

Many accountants—I would guess the large majority—feel they are relegated to only being pushers of information and recording transactions. They do not feel they are a player in improving decision making in their company at any level.

Whether you are in accounting at a manufacturer or a service provider, the need for understanding how actions can influence financial outcomes is critical. Hoping for good results is not enough. Hoping for improvement is not enough. Taking action with the knowledge that there is a better way and moving forward with confidence to provide innovative, valuable feedback on results will, in turn, influence better and better results. This is how you can become a Value Add Accountant.

Lean is The Best Way to Drive Organizational Value Creation

1

The Profit Model

When most people are asked what Lean is, they respond that it is a way to reduce waste or reduce costs. Some people who are focused on reducing employee costs regularly joke that Lean is an acronym for "Less Employees Are Needed." As negative and cynical as that sounds, it is not entirely wrong, though it does ignore all the growth opportunities—and employees needed—that are created by all the waste reduction. That attitude is terribly misplaced and ironic since employees are actually the source of all waste reduction improvement results in a sustaining Lean culture!

Lean activities create value. You might think only about creating value as related to direct product or service creation. Lean tools and events do, in fact, enhance a product directly in cost reduction, higher quality, shorter delivery time, etc. But additionally, conducting Lean activity across every company function and process favorably impacts these same issues since all activity in a well-run company ultimately should be taken to improve the product and customer experience.

Cost reduction is one aspect of creating value, and obviously, one primary motivation for reducing costs is a desire to reduce loss or increase profits. So, if not solely on the tossed-out backs of ex-employees, how else can value be created and profits increased?

This chapter discusses the relationship between value, profit, employees, and Lean activities.

As in any economic evaluation of business performance, there are five main drivers of value creation.

- Reduce cost

- Increase capacity

- Increase demand

- Improve variable margin percentage

- Reduce capital structure

Each of these drivers is positively impacted by well thought out Lean efforts. As a Value Add Accountant, it is important and sustaining to drive efforts to connect the Lean activities with value creation.

Figure 1 shows a view of the Profit Model, that is a key tool for evaluating Lean efforts in your company, and, which, reveals the relationship between the value creation drivers.

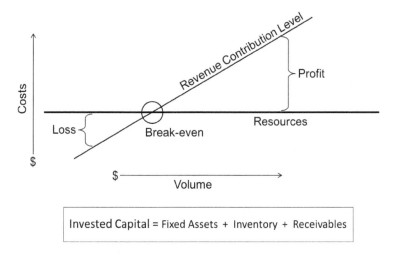

Figure 1 The Profit Model

In the Profit Model, there are two main dimensions. First, the thick horizontal line, Resources, represents the costs of a company. It is the total of all costs based on management decisions. These are the costs that do not vary with volume. This view is far different from the traditional ways of categorizing costs in financial statement (as discussed in the next chapter). In later chapters, we will go at length about how to evaluate if a cost is direct or shared.

The second dimension, Revenue Contribution Level, is the solid, sloped line, and represents the variable or contribution margin of items sold. The angle of the line is equivalent to the variable margin percentage of products at different levels of volume.

An example calculation of the variable margin is:

Sales Value	$100,000
Variable Costs	$ 25,000
Variable Margin	$ 75,000
Variable Margin %	75%

To plot this on the profit model you would move right to a volume level of $100,000, and then move upward to a variable margin of $75,000.

Also keep in mind, the total operational capital for most companies is the total of fixed assets, inventory, and accounts receivable (Figure 1).

5 DRIVERS OF ECONOMIC VALUE CREATION

The Profit Model reveals the relationships between the five drivers of economic value creation (EVC). They are:

Reduce Cost: When costs are reduced at a set volume, the difference between the margin and cost lines is increased which improves profitability.

Create Capacity: When the available capacity of existing people, facilities, and equipment is improved, it increases the opportunity to meet increased demand with existing resources.

Increase Demand: When demand increases, volume to customers grows resulting in an increase in variable margin.

Improve Variable Margin Percentage: When the relationship between sales price and variable costs increases, the slope of the line increases showing an increase in profit at a specific volume.

Reduce Capital Structure: When the capital resources needed at a specific volume are decreased, return on invested capital is improved.

If you think this sounds like an economic text, you are right. This is the basic economic value equation. While this book is not intended to be an economics lesson, it is important to know that Lean creates value not in some magical or flavor-of-the-month based way, but in solid economic value as measured historically and traditionally.

Lean is not a religion. It is not a dubious activity. It is eccentric given the static state of corporate accounting for the past 100 years. Most importantly, Lean is a solid way to drive improved, sustainable value. This is something accountants should be interested in and support as a valid and legitimate way to run a business.

The next sections look at specific examples where Lean directly affects the profit model drivers.

REDUCE COST

When costs are reduced at a set volume, the difference between the margin and cost (Resources) lines is increased which improves profitability (Figure 2).

When most people think of Lean, waste reduction is the element that first comes to mind. Less labor and capital is required when less wasteful activity is built into your processes. A cost reduction is when an actual real cost of the business is eliminated. The company no longer pays for it.

Some concrete examples include:

- Eliminating (or reducing) the need to pay an expediting charge to get products to customers when production is late.

- Eliminating materials used in replacing a defective product.

- Eliminating shipping costs for returned and replacement goods.

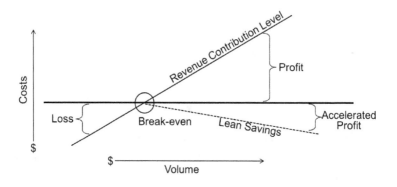

Figure 2 The Profit Model: Reduce Costs

- Not refilling a position when a person resigns due to increased internal labor capacity.

- Overtime eliminated due to less time required to complete tasks.

- Reducing payments for warehouse space, production space, equipment and tools because less is needed.

- Reducing financial complexity in the cost system which leads to reduced audit fees.

As part of one of Lantech's Lean process improvement events, the accounting team audited the external contracts to ensure the company was getting what it paid for.

On one contract, Lantech paid monthly for warehouse space needed to store periodically used equipment. The contract called for a fee based on the square footage used. An accounting team member and an operations partner visited the warehouse. They found that the actual space being used had dropped to less than half that which was being paid for. They corrected the contract and reduced Lantech's real cost every month going forward.

Often people think all changes that are beneficial also reduce cost, but this is not always the case even with some highly beneficial changes. I have heard the two following examples mistakenly thought of as cost reduction several times.

1. **Reducing setup time:**
    This by itself does not reduce a cost. Many are confused because at their company they talk about the "cost" of setup. They might even put a cost of setup in product cost. This is a frequently used way to assign or allocate costs to a product that are made in batches. And, while reducing setup is an absolutely critical improvement, it does not reduce cost per se. It actually increases available capacity, which is economic value creator number two.

2. **Eliminating activity with no change in resources:**
    For instance, a better layout is implemented which reduces the space between two operations. So, operators walk less to achieve a task. This is good. But, if the overall working time is not reduced, there is no cost change. It's another great improvement that creates additional capacity.

In summary, a reduced cost means you will no longer be paying for something you paid for in the past. You will happily encounter this often as you implement Lean improvements.

CREATE CAPACITY

When capacity of existing people, facilities, and equipment is raised, it increases the opportunity to meet increased demand with existing resources (Figure 3). Without a doubt, you will create available capacity as a result of improvements made in your Lean events more often than any other value creation driver.

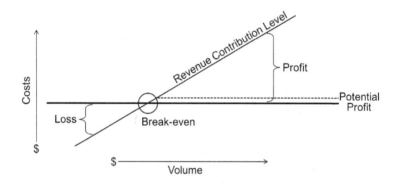

Figure 3 The Profit Model: Create Capacity

As an accountant, it is easy to be dismissive and, perhaps, shortsighted by saying, "Well, if the change does not appear on the financial statement, you haven't really done anything." And, that's true if you do not ever take the next step. Sure enough, then you will never reap the incredible benefits of creating capacity.

Below are four examples of capacity with suggestions of how to turn this capacity into financial impact.

Reduce Setup time: When you reduce setup time, you unlock capacity in machine availability for production and worker time. This freed up machine time can be used two ways. First, you can produce more to meet increased customer demand without needing more equipment. Second, you can reduce the batch size of products built which reduces WIP and finished goods inventory. Using the profit model, reduced setup time creates the opportunity for accelerated profit and a reduction in inventory.

Reduce space needed to produce service/product: This is achieved by co-location or right sizing work area and tools. That, in turn, creates space capacity which allows you to grow without adding facilities.

Reduce quality defects in product or service: This lowers rework, the time and resources needed to identify and correct defects.

Reduce worktime waste: The basis of kaizen improvement events is reforming an unlimited variety of your processes, and, thereby, discovering and eliminating wasteful steps. This frees up time that workers can use for other work. Plus, your company can maximize this benefit by providing workers with higher value work. This often creates a need for training and altered policies and practices to create or continue a safe environment, but results in a better, happier, and higher value work force.

Capacity creation of people's time is a critical element of value creation in the Lean organization, and the "Generating Profit Using Lean" chapter delves deeper into it.

INCREASE DEMAND

When demand increases, volume to customers increases. This results in an increase in variable margin (Figure 4).

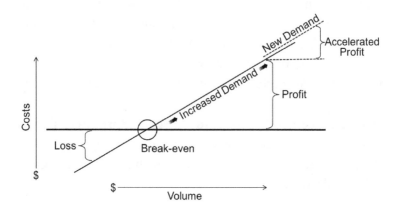

Figure 4 The Profit Model: Increase Demand

Launching growth initiatives while also driving Lean improvements is a perfect symbiotic match. On the profit side, it means there will be increased demand which can be met utilizing the capacity created which, in turn, increases profit and profit margin. On the people side, there is increased motivation to create capacity within one's own job when there are well-communicated and visual growth initiatives that will increase demand and the amount of work available...without having to work harder!

All companies want to increase demand. There is a much higher likelihood of this occurring when using Lean thinking because Lean improves the fundamental reasons a customer wants your company's product and services: prompt availability, customization, great customer service, first time quality, and lower cost.

There are many, many examples of how Lean supports each of these areas. The following examples discuss a few.

Prompt Availability: Lean helps reduce lead time by reducing the unnecessary steps in a process.

There was a kaizen event I facilitated that had a scope from "receipt of an order" through "when the order is sent to distribution for picking." It had a cross-functional team and was at a stock goods manufacturer. Each of the process steps was evaluated from the process map they built.

Immediate improvements in order entry were identified and implemented. The credit process was improved with benefits in order entry speed and accounting productivity. Opportunities in simplifying the part number process were identified and improved during a subsequent event.

And for a longer term strategic opportunity, the need to create an improved online order portal was identified. The resulting portal became a strategic initiative. The eventual improvement from this event was 90% of orders were provided to distribution the same day as received and over 50% within 1 hour. This reduced overall lead time by 5 days.

Customization: When customers can get a product or service the special way they want it without significant upcharge, it creates competitive advantage and customer loyalty.

I worked with a packaging equipment manufacturer who offered the customer a custom color for their machine. When the color option was requested, there was either a significant upcharge, or production chaos ensued that put meeting the committed shipment date at huge risk. At that time, they painted parts in batches and kept them on the shelf. Coordinating a different color for all the various parts was very time consuming, and if a part was forgotten, then it would delay production often resulting in overtime cost.

When the company changed to Lean thinking using one piece flow, all the parts for the special color could be painted at the same time with little disruption or forgotten parts. The customer was willing to pay an upcharge for the special service, and the company was comfortable with accepting the order and delivery date with confidence.

Far too many people think Lean is just for standard products. Nothing could be further from the truth. In fact, over 90% of the companies I have assisted over the past 12 years have customized products and services!

Great Customer Service: Another example has to do with the customization of customer service and addresses two fundamental customer "wants" at once.

A trailer company I worked with for a long time originally had one order entry, one engineering, and one purchasing department servicing all three of their product lines (normally referred to as "value streams" in the Lean community) within manufacturing. All order entry was the same whether the trailer was a simple repeatable trailer or a highly custom engineered one. A simple trailer order entry would wait it's turn behind a complex trailer order.

The company split order entry, engineering, and purchasing to match the product lines creating three complete value streams.

Then for the simple product line, the credit and deposit processes were simplified resulting in improved lead time and an easier business-to-customer relationship.

Through a lot of Lean improvement efforts, this product

line was eventually able to be offered through distributors with a simple configurator allowing pricing locally in the field. The features/options of the simple line were also focused on the usual items customers want.

Any order with options outside those items moved the order to the second value stream. That value stream had a slightly more complex order entry, engineering and purchasing process. The lead time was somewhat longer, and pricing was more and in alignment with the complexity.

The third value stream was for highly complex, project managed orders with significantly more upfront customer support and approval processes. By customizing each value stream to the need of the customer, each type of customer received the process, pricing and lead time expected. Today their company is a leader in the custom trailer industry.

First Time Quality: It may be obvious, but customers are happiest when the product or service they purchase is correct when first received. This goes for off-the-shelf, custom, and all the rest.

Lower Cost: When a company's costs are reduced, they may pass this on to their customers via a lower price (cost for their customer!). Improved product performance can also reduce the customer's cost through less employee time spent on incoming inspection of parts, resolving incorrect paperwork, dealing with warranty issues, etc.

IMPROVE VARIABLE MARGIN PERCENTAGE

When the relationship between sales price and variable costs increases, the slope of the revenue contribution line increases, increasing profit at a specific volume (Figure 5).

There are mainly three ways to improve the variable margin of a product:

- Increase sales price

- Reduce material content

- Reduce cost of materials

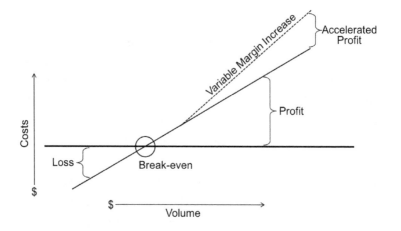

Figure 5 The Profit Model: Improve Variable Margin Percentage

"Material" in this discussion refers to all the variable costs providing a product or service. This typically includes raw materials, purchased parts, variable utilities, commissions, and shipment costs. Variable margin is discussed more in the "Options for Lean Management Accounting Statements" chapter.

Increase Sales Price: Lean improvement helps increase price by reducing the barriers that many sales people face when discussing a price increase. If the product today has poor quality or long lead times, it is very hard to get customer agreement on a price increase. If there are no areas of customer loyalty thanks to customization, it is difficult to price products higher than your direct competition. So, price improvements often accompany the related Lean driven improvements in product quality, lead time, and service offerings.

Reduce Material Content: Reductions in the amount of material content used is often achieved through avoiding errors in the production process, a common target of Lean thinking, by building in quality at the source.

Or, Lean improvements in product design that utilize materials more effectively and encourage working with material suppliers can reduce content. One specific example exposed by Lean process analysis came from purchasing materials in the mode or shape needed rather than buying common materials and then shaping or cutting them to size locally.

Reduce Cost of Materials: Reductions in material price is the third way to adjust variable margin. So, if your improvement event concerns materials, the group may well find themselves working with suppliers and engineers to ensure the specifications of the materials do not exceed the customer demand. If a material that is not customer facing is of a quality spec greater than the need, the price of the material will normally cost more than necessary. Further, by increasing standardization of your materials through Lean efforts, the quantity purchased may increase rewarding you with improved pricing.

For instance, a company that prints envelopes purchased another company with similar products. At the purchased company, a wide variety of colors were offered with significant steps on color matching.

However, the original company had a much smaller color palette. When working with customers, they determined the wide variety of colors were not a competitive option. By reducing the color options, ink cost was reduced.

The Value Add Accountant can be extremely valuable in helping to get better clarity into the components of variable margin. Really understanding variable margin by product line can also dramatically improve the Value Add Accountant's ability to improve profit forecasting based on future demand.

REDUCE CAPITAL STRUCTURE

When the capital resources needed at a specific volume are decreased, this improves return on invested capital.

The capital structure of most companies has many elements (Figure 6), but the three most prominent are inventory, accounts receivable, and fixed assets/PPE (property, plant and equipment). Lean can have a huge impact of these three elements.

Inventory: With the adoption of one piece flow and pull production, the first significant observed gain will be a natural reduction in work in process (WIP) inventory. This pleases accountants too because when WIP reduces, the job of valuing WIP inventory is simplified.

WIP reduction was one of my first insights that led me to eliminating standard cost accounting as CFO. If the WIP is low and stable, accounting did not need a complex costing system to identify valuation. *Real Numbers* thoroughly covers the inherent problems with Standard Cost accounting.

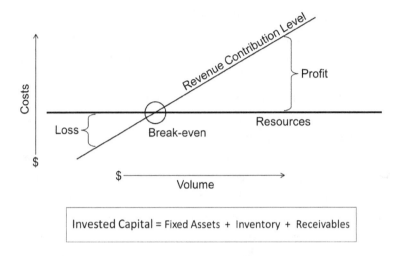

Figure 6 The Profit Model: Reduce Capital Structure

The other direct benefit of one piece flow and pull production is the reduction in lead time throughout the process. With a reduction in lead time, the need for finished goods inventory reduces and may even be eliminated. If using MRP, this reduction will only happen if the inventory planners recognize this lead time improvement in their EOQ (Economic Order Quantity) or safety stock calculations.

Raw Materials should also have a dramatic reduction as Lean visual management and the use of kanban tools are implemented for the replenishment of raw materials. I have found this to be one of the most underutilized changes that can have a dramatic impact of capital structure. In *Easier Simpler and Faster*[6], you can find more information about applying kanban to replenishment.

Accounts Receivable: Next is the impact of Lean on accounts receivable. Groups I've worked with have found it very revealing to use Lean tools to look deeply into why customers do not pay their invoices in full or in a timely manner. In my experience, about 50% of all open accounts can be reduced without turning to the age old (and often incorrect) gripe of blaming the customer and demanding faster payment!

There are two main activities that will help you really understand the Lean opportunity within accounts receivable. One is to schedule a kaizen event covering the process from order intake through recording the customer payment. As part of this event, the attendees will create a detailed process map. This map will help the kaizen team see opportunities (probably many) to reduce the time to get the invoice created and sent to the customer. A very achievable goal is for the invoice to arrive at the customer location within the same day (or even hour). All data for the invoice can be known before the need to invoice.

During the kaizen, you can setup your process to be able to quickly ascertain which customers are willing to pay promptly, but the payment has not been submitted because of some type of error in the invoice process. For instance, most invoicing systems assign invoice numbers sequentially. If a customer who has multiple invoices skips over an invoice number, it is a sure sign of a looming problem. Identifying this gap and addressing it before it gets old will improve your capital assigned to accounts receivable.

The second main activity to utilize with accounts receivable is defects. They do not reduce accounts receivable directly, but over time it will have a very positive impact. I found most defects were in our process and had often been blamed on the customer forever. In the chapter, "Using Defects to Drive Financial Gain," the use of accounts receivable defects will guide you to many, many upstream problems that affect the customer as well as inflate the capital structure.

There's evidence of defects you might want to ponder every time a customer:

- pays a different amount than the amount listed on the invoice,

- pays for fewer quantity than invoiced,

- pays a different price than invoiced, and

- does not pay an expedite charge

This is a short list of the many avoidable, 100% waste defects that accounts receivable transactions have before they have been through Lean improvement activities.

It's not from anyone's lack of trying or focus. It's from no one individual seeing and understanding the entire process and making what turn out to be false assumptions just to get the job done. We all do it. This is an area that the Value Add Accountant can and should take the lead in organizationally. Everyone the process touches in your company will be thankful you did.

Fixed Assets or Plant, Property, and Equipment (PPE): The last element of reducing capital structure is the PPE of the organization: the buildings, the vehicles, the equipment, the computers. All the stuff you buy to support the work of the people. Lean can dramatically lower the amount of PPE you need.

You will reduce the space you need to hold all the things the company owns that are not currently moving like inventory, records, even next year's holiday decorations! Space previously filled with racks and sophisticated control cages will be freed up for productive activities.

Space for inventory and for people can be held at a constant and often even lowered based on all the improvements mentioned above.

Additional changes can be seen when equipment and tools are right sized for the actual flow of customer demand.

For instance, one company had a large saw to handle all the cutting of the panels for a product. It was high powered and could cut many panels at one time. There was significant planning to ensure all the materials for all the parts to be cut together were available at the needed time. The equipment was large and expensive because it had to be able to handle many different cutting heads and types of materials. It also had to be very fast to cut all the parts needed in a day. Parts were cut at the convenience of the saw schedule and put into inventory (space and process waste) until they were needed for the customer order.

In the Lean world, this type of equipment used for many products and often a gate to a product's manufacturing schedule, is called a "monument." Once value streams were established by the company, it was more effective to have more, smaller, and less sophisticated saws that cut the materials as needed for a given customer order. These saws typically cost far less than the large saw and capacity (more saws) could be added in much smaller increments with minimal cost. The monument was gone, and production flow was greatly enhanced.

At the very least, compare the actual rate of customer demand for a machine to its actual use. In the Lean community this is called a "takt time versus cycle time comparison." Often, processes using the equipment have not optimized the equipment capability, or there is more production than is actually needed. As Orest Fiume says, "Takt is NOT just a manufacturing thing!"

TRADITIONAL KEY METRICS

Up to now, this chapter has not talked about the traditional accounting language of key metrics of the company? Does that mean they are obsolete in the Lean world? No. An emphatic "No."

The profit model is just an additional arrow in your reporting quiver. And, it is an important one to understand the financial aspect of Lean.

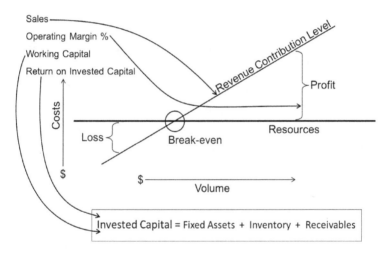

Figure 7 The Profit Model: Traditional Outcome Linkage

In fact, the profit model links very nicely to some of the most common key performance indicators (Figure 7).

- Net sales links with the increase in demand on the variable margin line.

- Profitability links with the difference between costs and variable margin.

- Working capital as a % of sales relates to two of the components of capital structure.

- Inventory turns is reflected in the variable cost and inventory factors.

- DSO relates to the sales and accounts receivable factors.

- Return on assets relates to the profit and the capital structure.

SUMMARY

The profit model is a visual tool set the Value Add Accountant can use with your employees, your managers, and your executives. The accelerated profit model (Figure 8), a composite view of the profit model element, displays—in conjunction with appropriate explanations—how Lean efforts can improve the financial performance of the company.

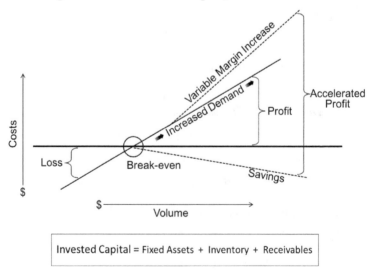

Figure 8 The Accelerated Profit Model

Lean is not a spooky, magical practice. It is a proven way to enhance near and long term financial outcomes of the company through focusing on customer need and employee genius.

As a Value Add Accountant, you have the opportunity and obligation to help translate and justify these improvements using the profit model as a template for communication.

2

Using Trends to Prove ROI

Evaluate and Promote Lean Improvement Activities

Accounting statements are the basis of reporting the financial results of a company's performance. Every accounting statement is based on the age-old method of creating double entry transactions to record information based on a system of standards called the Generally Accepted Accounting Principles or GAAP. The Financial Accounting Standards Board (FSB) maintains and occasionally amends GAAP for the U. S. private sector.

The accounting field has many tenets, standards, and concepts. They have been the basis for accepted practice for many decades. In spite of this extensive structure, there is one thing traditional accounting cannot do that is very important to every company's Lean journey and how it is approached.

That something is this. Accounting cannot measure something that does not happen.

A cornerstone of Lean thinking is to eliminate non-value add waste (as perceived by the customer). Eliminate means to make it not happen in the first place. Stop it. Avoid it. It means ending wasteful steps so employee work and expense can more often be put towards actions a customer will value.

The gains are obvious to those doing the work improved by Lean. They know they are doing the same work in less time with better results. So, Lean is reducing the labor required for existing work, but accounting has no way to record and report that positive, impactful fact.

So, Lean companies have a monster accounting conflict. On the one hand, there is a long accepted and virtually unquestioned accounting system that only records items that do happen. And on the other hand, you are adopting Lean, a proven waste reduction philosophy that aims to stop doing unnecessary things in the name of productivity, efficient use of resources, reducing space required, improving delivery time, reducing inventory, eliminating rework, and on and on and on.

Implementing Lean is going to add some amount of upfront costs that can be accounted for, but all the ongoing future labor saved and materials not needed because of not doing wasteful actions cannot be accounted for.

ROI AND LEAN

This causes a frequent management question that I and other Lean leaders receive, "What is the return on Lean thinking?" What is the return on investment? What is the payback? All of these questions include traditional financial phrases voiced when evaluating projects and investments. This question often stymies accounting professionals and managers who are used to answering this question based on their monthly, quarterly or annual financial statement.

The vast majority of positive, high value add changes from Lean are not shown on the traditional financial statement. The statement will not show the missing cost when no longer expediting for orders sent late or no longer expediting materials in for goods not on hand. Or, overtime not needed to hit a ship date, or the warehouse rental for space no longer needed for inventory.

You also will not see the wasted time to rework the order information that was incorrectly entered, or the waiting time to get approvals, or the time lost reviewing information several times. In fact, very little of the cost savings (costs not incurred) from the entire list of 8 types of waste eliminated by Lean activities (Table 1) will be found on the financial statements when those wastes are no longer there.

The 8 Wastes	
Defects	Anything not done properly the first time: rework, redo, adjustment, scrap, etc.
Over Production	Making more than is needed at the time: inventory, more information than is used, etc.
Waiting	People, machinery, or work stopped or not flowing.
Neglect of Human Talent	Safety risks, mind numbing work, unclear expectations, no time for improvement.
Transportation	The movement of work. Information moved from one system to another manually.
Inventory	Work that is stopped: raw materials, work in process (WIP), finished goods, in-baskets, etc.
Motion	Non-optimized or unneeded movement of the human body.
Excess Processing	Work not adding value (e.g. specifications tighter than requirements).

Table 1 The 8 Wastes

So, what is the Value Add Accountant to do to support the organization that is transforming to Lean thinking? Should you even try to answer the ROI question?

My professional experience suggests an inverse relationship between increasing deep knowledge of Lean thinking and the need for detailed financial justification. Lean thinkers know that you can go to the Lean workplace and see work flowing more smoothly with less defects.

As Figure 9 indicates, the greater the understanding of Lean thinking, the less need for financial justification.

But, what are the odds that every decision maker in your company is a Lean guru? Well, zero, at least for a while.

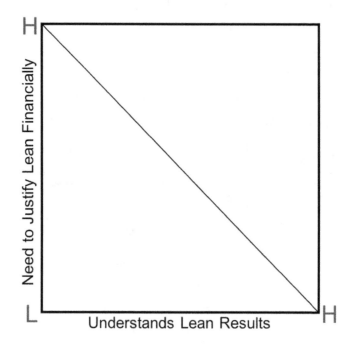

Figure 9 Justifying Lean

So, knowing the "score" is going to be important one way or another. Providing insightful information is also one way to show "Respect for People," and even the most devoted Lean manager will gladly take financial evidence whenever it is offered.

So, "Is there a way to attack the Lean/ROI question?" I have pondered this as a CFO as well as the many times I have been asked it as a consultant.

TREND METRICS

Through experiments, trial and error, and deep discussions with other financial professionals and Lean experts, I concluded that compiling and publishing trends is the best way to address the Lean ROI.

This means utilizing your company's historic trend data to determine how much positive change has occurred with your Lean experiments and improvements. What is the progress? How much value has been gained? How much contribution to profit has been achieved by Lean efforts? Has the company moved in the right direction? Is the company better than last year?

In effect, this means each company becomes their own benchmark. Progress is measured (and celebrated) relative to your previous position. Since the Lean journey at every company is unique to the current state of the company, and since Lean is not a mature methodology practiced and measured the same in every business, industry-based benchmarking would be difficult to impossible to utilize with Lean.

Similar to the multiple metrics in traditional financials statements, there can be multiple metrics used to measure and evaluate Lean progress. In general, business metrics can be either qualitative or quantitative measures.

Traditional financial reporting includes only quantitative metrics such as a statement or a metric. Lean trends reporting is also based on quantitative metrics. (It is important to note that outside the scope of this book are many high impact qualitative

Lean metrics used in manufacturing, hospitals, the Lean Office, and other businesses.)

How might trends be applied to help reveal the impact of Lean thinking on an organization?

The previous chapter described Lean benefits applied to the profit model including five ways to impact financial results. Those five categories can also identify macro trends that will help show the impact of your Lean efforts. They are:

- Reduce Cost

- Create capacity

- Increase demand

- Improve variable (contribution) margin percentage

- Reduce capital structure

At the broadest level, we could just look at the trend of a traditional metric like gross margin percentage or operating profit percentage. But there are many problems with these measures as described in *Real Numbers*[7].

The concept of a trend metric is to see how a particular measurable element quantitatively relates to another measurable element, and, then, to see how the relationship changes, for better or worse, over time. It does not mean that one element causes the other or is the result of the other.

"Learning by doing" is very powerful way to learn, so the rest of this chapter provides three examples of trend measures written so you can work through the example and calculate the measure using your own data.

METRIC EXAMPLE 1
Sales Per Employee Trend

A good example of a trend metric is Sales Per Employee. This is the trend of sales as related to the trend of the number of employees. It is one of the broadest metrics to reflect changes in a business in general, and it is very revealing of the high value of Lean efforts during times of growth. First the mechanics:

1. Assuming it is measured annually, use the "total year of sales." This can be found on the income statement.

2. Then identify the number of employees. Some analysts use the number of employees at the end of the year. Others like to use the number at the end of each month and average it. (Simple is good.) Two or more completed years of data are necessary.

3. Start with an example of a fictional company (or business unit) of $150 Million in sales for year two and 833 employees. Divide $150,000,000 by 833 and the result is a metric of $180,000.

    At this point, there is only a single, standalone metric. A trend must have two or more points to compare.

4. Next identify the sales in year one and employees for year one. For the example, let's use $100 Million and 800 employees. Divide $100,000,000 by 800 and the result is a metric of $125,000.

Now there is a trend: Sales Per Employee of $125,000 in year one and $180,000 in year two.

This is a very large improvement. And what does it mean in financial terms? What value does this have to the organization?

It means the company has found ways to recognize more sales without having to increase employee count at the same rate. Can a dollar value be put on this? Yes, the cost of the additional people who the company AVOIDED adding to payroll in support of this higher level of sales can be calculated.

5. First, calculate how many employees would have been needed at sales of $150 Million if our sales per employee was the same as year one, $125,000. Dividing $150,000,000 by $125,000 results in 1200 employees.

6. But in actuality, there were only 833 employees or an avoidance of 367 employees. Estimate the average cost of an employee, say $75,000. Now calculate the cost avoidance: 367 employees times $75,000 equals $27,525,000 saved (i.e. NOT SPENT).

In a Lean company, this savings is probably a direct result of reducing the 8 Wastes identified during Lean improvement activities.

Below is a summary of this example.

Sales Per Employee

- Year 1: $100 Million in sales ÷ by 800 employees = $125,000

- Year 2: $150 Million in sales ÷ by 833 employees = $180,000

- Financial Benefit: Savings in cost of additional employees (if sales per employee had not improved from $125,000 to $180,000)

- Calculate number of employees (if at old sales per employee rate): $150 Million ÷ by $125,000 = 1200 employees

- Avoidance of higher employee count: 1200 - 833 = 367 employees

- Cost per employee estimate: $75,000

- Savings: 367 × $75,000 = $27,525,000 a year!

Thinking back to the profit model, you can see that this measure utilizes two of the drivers of accelerated profit:

- **Increase Demand:** Sales increased from $100 Million to $150 Million.

- **Increase Capacity:** More employees and with improved productivity per employee verified by the improved Sales Per Employee metric of over $27 Million.

LOCALIZING SALES PER EMPLOYEE

Sales per Employee is one of my favorite high level, macro metrics across an entire company. I also want my client teams to have local metrics that they can directly identify with and impact.

The Sales Per Employee metric can be used at the local level as well. For instance, if you are a finance and accounting team supporting the full company (or business unit.), take the sales of the company/business unit and divide it by the number of finance/accounting employees for each year.

Here is an example:

- Year One: $100M sales divided by 8 employees = $12,500,000

- Year Two: $150M sales divided by 10 employees = $15,000,000

- Contribution to profit equals $150,000,000/$12,500,000 = 12 employees. Since there are only 10 employees, this is an avoidance of 2 employees at average of $75,000= $150,000.

Another way to localize is to connect to a revenue generating value stream. In this case, take the revenue specific to the value stream. Use only the employees that are directly assigned to the value stream (or a sub component). Don't try to allocate people from shared areas, just the areas that are directly managed by the value stream.

This way you can treat the value stream like a small mini-business and see directly how your improvement efforts are affecting the profit generating power of Lean!

A nice exercise for you would be to calculate this measure for your company or business unit. Draw the profit model and pencil the results in showing the increase sales demand and the accelerated profit benefit.

METRIC EXAMPLE 2
Cost Element as a % of Sales Trend

Another example of using trends to evaluate the benefits of waste elimination or improved resource utilization is to look at the trend of a cost element compared to the sales rate of the company.

The cost element could be any cost element that you are striving to eliminate or better utilize. It could be expediting costs, scrap, overtime, legal fees, worker compensation, etc.

For this example, use scrap of materials. The metric will be scrap as a percent (%) of sales.

1. Start with the scrap value and the sales of one period. Use one year for this example. Generally, you can find the scrap expense on the income statement as a line item on the chart of accounts. You may want to ask your cost analyst or controller to help you find this number if you do not have access or experience with the accounting information.

2. Assume year one scrap expense of $2.5 Million on sales of $100 Million. Divide the scrap expense by the sales. The metric, Scrap as a % of Sales equals 2.5%.

3. Assume year two scrap expense of $2.1 Million on sales of $150 Million. The calculation for Scrap as a % of Sales equals 1.4%.

You can see an amazing trend with a reduction from 2.5% of sales to 1.4% of sales. Now calculate cost avoidance.

4. As in the first example, convert this to the total avoided cost by calculating the scrap expense at the year two sales level by the year one scrap rate. Multiply year two sales $150 Million times .025 (2.5%) for a total of $3.75 Million.

5. Subtract the $2.1 Million actual from the $3.75 Million for a cost avoidance or savings of $1.65 Million.

Below is a summary of this example.

Scrap as a % of Sales

- Year 1: $2.5 Million of scrap ÷ by $100 Million in sales = 2.5%

- Year 2: $2.1 Million of scrap ÷ by $150 Million in sales = 1.4%

- Financial Benefit: Lower cost of scrap (if rate had not decreased from 2.5% to 1.4%)

- Calculate old cost of scrap (if at new sales): $150 Million × 2.5% = $3.75 M

- Savings: $3.75 Million – $2.1 Million = $1,650,000 a year!

On the profit model, this metric reveals a cost reduction when implementing improvements that lead to a cost reduction of scrap.

You can use this same calculation with many, many different cost elements. For instance, materials % of sales might be a good indicator of improvements in the revenue variable margin on the profit model. Another example might be using a balance sheet account item such as inventory or accounts receivable as a % of sales. These would be indicators of the opportunities to reduce the capital structure of the business.

METRIC EXAMPLE 3
Common Trend

Another way to identify the financial value of Lean is to use a common metric and then show the dollar values difference.

In this example, use Days Sales Outstanding (DSO) as the metric. DSO is the common metric for describing the trend of accounts receivable as it relates to sales. DSO is often reported, but the important way in which it relates to cash and the balance sheet is often not considered.

1. Start with the DSO of two time periods. It is important that you use annual (or annualized) information since the measures include both income statement and balance sheet elements.

2. You also need the sales total for both of the same time periods.

3. In this example for year 1, use a DSO of 60 days and sales of $100 Million. For year 2, use a DSO of 55 days and sales of $150 Million.

4. Calculate the receivables for year 2 (or get directly from the balance sheet if available). The receivables for year 2 is $150 Million/360 days in a year times 55 days DSO which equals $22.9 Million.

5. Then for year 1 when the receivables were 60 days, the balance avoided is $150 Million/360 days times 60 days which equals $25 Million or an improvement of $2.1 Million of funds available.

   - If the funds were applied to a reduction of debt, then there would also be a direct savings. If the interest rate is 4%, then $2.1 Million times .04 equals $84,000 savings of interest not paid.

   - If the funds are used for investments and the cost of capital is 12%, then ($2.1 Million times .12) $252,000 is equivalent annual contribution to ROI.

Below is a summary of this example.

DSO

- Year 1: Sales = $100 Million, DSO = 60 days, A/R = $100 Million ÷ 360 days × 60 = $16.7 Million

- Year 2: Sales = $150 Million, DSO = 55 days, A/R = $150 Million ÷ 360 days × 55 = $22.9 Million

- If Year 2 DSO had been 60, then A/R = $150 Million ÷ 360 × 60 = $25 Million

- Improved Cash Balance = $25 Million – $22.9 Million = $2.1 Million

- **Savings:** If applied to debt and the interest rate = 4%, then $2.1 Million × .04 = $84,000

- **Investment Opportunities:** If Cost of Capital = 12%, then $2.1M × .12 = $252,000

From the Profit Model perspective, this is a reduction in the capital structure just as if done as a % of Sales but using a more common metric.

SUMMARY

As you can see, there are many quantitative metrics that can be used as trend indicators to help identify the value of your Lean efforts. When presented in an appropriate context, they can be powerful allies in justifying Lean improvement activities and fuel for driving future Lean events.

Your imagination is the only limit of how to use these and other metrics to help describe the cost savings and other benefits of work, time or activity that has been eliminated by Lean improvement activities.

Showing trends is a Value Add Accountant staple.

3

Generating Profit Using Lean

A lot of people just starting their Lean journey or who only have used Lean tools superficially say, "I don't see the financial value of Lean." or "I don't see how reducing the 8 Wastes has a financial impact."

This chapter will address those concerns and suggest how you can optimize financial gains with Lean.

Adopting Lean principles and tools will positively impact your company and its bottom line primarily in three overarching ways.

- You will focus on creating customer value with your products and services.

- You will reduce the wait times between transactions and activities.

- You will deploy the capacity of your people towards higher value work.

Customer value and wait times are directly addressed every time a company uses Lean methods and tools. They're eliminating or shortening non-value add steps within a process. They're striving to eliminate waste, and wait time is pure waste. And, in so doing, they're freeing up your people to have available capacity. If your company is implementing a lot of Lean-based changes, they are freeing up a lot of capacity.

But, do management and decision makers realize this? If John and Camila have 200 less touches and 6 hours less wait time during the month because of recent kaizen improvements, will management know that? Others will have been affected this way as well. And, if decision makers do realize it, what are they going to do about it?

As a key component of Lean financial impact, this chapter will show you how to turn available capacity into a financial gain for your company and a workplace win for your employees.

CAPACITY AND VALUE

If you think back to the profit model (Figure 10), one of the five main ways of creating financial value is capacity creation. The large majority of the waste you eliminate with Lean thinking is going to create newly available capacity in the form of human capability and time. Creating capacity in and of itself doesn't raise your company's financial value. It is what is done with the newly available capacity that will or will not provide greater value in the future.

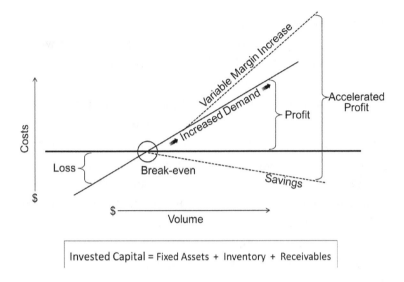

Figure 10 The Accelerated Profit Model

If you want to increase value, you need to figure out how to redeploy the released capacity with high value work. One of the ways to do that is to move people around. In other words, use them in additional or different ways than currently.

Keep in mind, that all the waste that is eliminated consists of non-value add elements in the form of duplication, producing unused output, defects, needless repetition, low efficiency, etc. (The 8 Wastes, Mura, Muri). In addition to being non-value add, this most often means you've eliminated tasks that are uninteresting at best and mind numbing at worst.

As a result, employees expect their jobs to evolve and change for the better in companies where Lean activities affect change ongoing. Some are even given an opportunity for an entire career shift. My experience suggests that most employees—but, not all—thrive in the ever-evolving environment created by Lean.

WAIT AND SEE

Before discussing ways to deploy this capacity, consider why a company can't just wait for this capacity to be deployed over time (other than it is wasteful and inefficient).

First, remember that the company had purposely used Lean thinking, creativity, and experimentation to discover the ways to (1) eliminate tasks, (2) do tasks quicker, or (3) do tasks right the first time so rework and inspection is not needed. The employees have participated in this effort and are happy to have eliminated non-value add work, but also are keenly aware that, going forward, less work needs to be done.

Most managers think, "Well, let's just grow into this freed up capacity." Yes! That is a great and necessary thing to do during your Lean journey. If you are going to launch Lean as a strategy, then also launch growth strategies.

If you do not have growth strategies, employees will be cynical when you tell them they will not lose their employment based on Lean. They will see and feel the capacity being created because it will be obvious to them that there is less to do with so much process waste eliminated. And, they will worry that they or their associates will be at risk of being laid off. If layoffs have been an approach to reducing costs in the past, employees have very good reason to feel that it will happen again…even if you tell them it will not.

Further, you will not grow into the capacity by simply waiting…at least not the way the work is currently allocated in many areas. If the work is just simplified (i.e. less time to do the same work), then growing into the capacity could work somewhat. But let's say you reduce some work by 50%. How long will it take to grow into that? And, maybe the work in another area is simplified by 25%, then any future growth will absorb that capacity at a different rate.

For work that was completely eliminated, or where the rework component was eliminated, that work is 100% gone. You will never need to do that work again. You will not grow into it. And, of course, you do not want to grow into something that should not be done in the first place.

If you wait too long, the current work will begin to expand to fill the available time. Why? Because every employee knows it is important to be busy. This is an axiom everyone learns during their work life. So being without work to do is not a positive state, and the appearance of work being done will fill any time voids. No one has ever gotten excited about saying on their performance review, "I had excess time!"

MOVE TO HIGHER VALUE ACTIVITIES

To reap the benefit of this new capacity, you will either need to move existing valuable work to the people with freed up capacity or move the people with freed up time to the valuable work. And the sooner the better!

Here are some of the ways you can proactively use newly available capacity:

- **Move to open jobs:** Use people with available capacity to fill higher value positions open within your company. Filling the role, may require one move or perhaps multiple moves to get a person to the position. Or, it may mean moving portions of the open roles to people that have capacity created.

  For example, if you have freed up time in material handling and you have work open in procurement, you could move a portion of the material replenishment work to the material handler to avoid needing to fill a "procurement" role.

- **Move to strategic activities:** Many Lean companies use strategic deployment planning, a Lean method used to create focus on key strategic initiatives that are meant to move the company toward the vision or "true north" goals of the company.

  Too often these initiatives are divvied up between a variety of people to work on along with their "normal" roles which can easily run into priority negligence.

  A better way is to take someone with available capacity and move that person into a temporary assignment to work part or full time on an initiative. There are two benefits. First, the initiative will be completed sooner. Second, the person deployed to the initiative will build additional skills and capability.

- **Move to value creation opportunities:** Where are there needs for work that influences the customer demand rate, reduces costs, or improves asset utilization—all high value activities?

  It might be in areas where the need does not require a full time, permanent role, and, so the work is rarely or ever done. You can probably think of work that you know will be beneficial but gets put off over and over because "everyone is busy."

  This type of work might be the perfect part time role for someone with available capacity. Examples might include creating customer contact calls (pre or post sales), survey opportunities, or cleanup of physical or information areas. There are countless other possibilities.

- **Insource**: Identify work that is currently being out-sourced. It could include sub-contractors, component manufacturing, training, maintenance, etc. Consider moving all or part of the work internal which may have benefits of cost reduction, quicker lead time and small batch size opportunity. Not to mention the positive impact on your employees upon hearing about the insourcing!

- **Switch jobs within the department**: As a way to deepen and broaden the skills of a team, switching jobs can be a great way to take advantage of freed up capacity. Who on the team is overloaded or needed for other tasks? Move time to that area to reduce the backlog of work, to improve skills, and also create some fresh eyes on the work that may result in further improvement, waste elimination and capacity creation.

- **Promote and move the leader**: Consider not only moving around the direct worker who has new capacity, but also those in supervisory or management roles. Moving the leader and having a staff member step up permanently or temporarily to fill the roll, will also deepen skills in the team. The leader may be then utilized for their own strategic or value creating opportunity.

- **Lean champion role**: Create a role to drive future improvement activities within your team. This might be as simple as creating a huddle leader, or it might mean actually moving a person to your Lean or Operational Excellence (OE) team for their development.

If your company has only recently started their Lean journey, and does not yet have an OE office, a high potential individual with freed up capacity and an interest in process improvement might be a perfect candidate to help start that office.

I have noticed that the most effective Lean champions nearly always come from within a company. Plus, the Lean champions often become the most qualified leaders for the future.

The "move" you apply in any given situation will depend on the amount of available capacity, the roles and individuals involved, and the current company environment.

When you decide to move people, select the people with the most potential to grow and develop. This isn't always easy for the current supervisor/manager to offer out of fear of diminishing the capability of their team. But when the people with greater potential are selected, it results in career and organization development. Plus, it signals to the entire organization that moving to new opportunities is an honor and positive recognition.

BARRIERS

A Value Add Accountant will want to support and encourage these higher value moves. To do so, you may need to stop or modify traditional activities that can act as barriers to them.

- **Budgets**: Budgets and Lean action are diametrically opposed.

  Traditionally and typically today, an annual budget is created 2-3 months prior to an upcoming year and then locked in.

  In Lean environments, there is a continuous focus

on improvements: engaging employees to find and make improvements, strategy improvements, and value stream or process improvements. It is impossible to know in advance how those improvements will impact the business and collectively their impact may well be significant over a year.

Therefore, it is impossible to budget and include Lean improvement impact with any degree of precision.

If the budget is a strong factor in evaluating company performance, then managers will be restricted in their ability to move people around because the move will not mesh with the budget.

To address this dichotomy, the Value Add Accountant will need to either adjust the budget (with a lot of non-value add work) or loosen the expectation on the specific areas of budget performance.

Some Lean companies eliminated the budget and now use a rolling forecast instead.

- **Posting jobs:** Some companies require posting jobs before filling them to allow all employees an equal opportunity to pursue growth opportunities. In general, that is a great idea. However, if you have freed up resources, you should give them priority on filling open jobs.

  Communicating to the company in advance that the standard posting policy will be excepted for moving people around is a good idea. It answers questions that will arise because of the exception, and it indirectly promotes participation in improvement efforts as everyone sees those who have been freed up getting opportunities.

- **Projects and initiatives**: Think through how you will monitor resources on strategic projects and initiatives. Do you want to move costs to a project? Do you want to reward cost centers for moving resources to temporary assignments?

  If so, you will need a way to assure teams that if a person's compensation is moved to a project, when they return, there will not be a penalty for showing a large percentage increase in spending from year to year. It might be easier to leave the person's compensation in their home department to avoid this issue.

- **A capacity cost department**: If a role is able to be completely removed from a department, you will want to move the person's compensation to another costing location so that the originating department is "rewarded" for the cost reduction.

  Create a department where the pay for these persons can be assigned until they are redeployed. The cost in this new department can be a signal to management of the success of creating capacity as well as an indicator of people available for redeployment.

- **Compensation**: Moving people around to new assignments often creates the opportunity for additional training requirements, and the pay of the person and the new role may not be in alignment.

  You will want to think about how to handle these issues policy wise and communicate any policy change to employees. Personal compensation is definitely a concern for everyone when employees are moved around.

Here is an example of how you might design and communicate your strategy on these compensation issues:

1. Employee who are freed up from their current roles due to productivity improvements will not lose their employment. (This is a Lean axiom.)

2. In making this commitment, the company will need to reassign new work to employees.

3. If the new work is significantly outside an employee's current compensation rate, then the employee will be in the position for a defined evaluation period.

4. After the evaluation period, the employee's compensation will be changed to a relevant pay range.

If the employee is under the relevant pay range, they will be brought to the minimum of the range.

If the employee is over the maximum of the range, they will stay at their pay for 24 months, and then pay will be adjusted to the top of the new range. Every effort will be made to assist the employee to move to a job closer to their current pay range during the 24 months.

WHERE'S THE MONEY

So far, this chapter has provided you with several ideas on how to address newly available capacity, what the advantages are, and how to avoid common pitfalls.

But, how are you going to justify these changes in dollars to your boss and the C-suite who think in those terms a lot? Perhaps you will use the profit model (Figure 11) to demonstrate the re-deployment of resources will impact financial outcomes.

The Sales per Employee metric was introduced in Chapter 2. This one metric can be the primary indicator of how well rede-ployment of people to value add work is impacting the company.

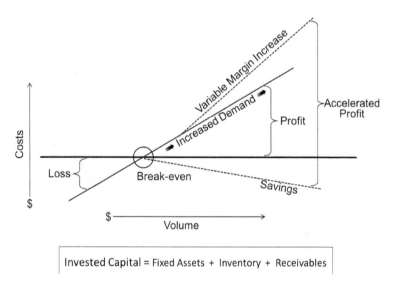

Figure 11 The Accelerated Profit Model

SUMMARY

As a Value Add Accountant, try to adopt the mindset that any employee time that becomes available due to improvement can be freely deployed to the best advantage. Thereby, you should strive in every way possible to move that time and genius of the employees in your company to higher value work.

Though it might take some time to fully see it in companies

just adopting Lean, these moves are a long-term positive experience for organizational development and for employee career growth and development. This truly represents "Continuous improvement with respect for people."—a Lean tenet—with the outcome of converting freed up capacity to real financial value.

Most seasoned Lean leaders including myself have stories of employees who once given opportunities through capacity creation to change their job and/or career went on to remarkable, unexpected success for both them and the company.

That's a big value add all the way around.

SECTION II

Leveraging Finance and Accounting Information

4

Close the Books

The Lean principles of waste elimination, quality at the source, and providing product based on customer demand are each a critical element in reducing the time to close the financial books on a monthly basis.

Money is the language of business, and no single report tells the money story better than the monthly income statement and balance sheet. Providing that information quickly, reliably, and accurately should be an improvement target in your company.

Utilizing breakthrough kaizen events is the fastest and best way to reduce overtime and rework in the monthly close process. A kaizen event is a quick change, action-oriented process improvement session where a cross-functional team analyzes the "current state" and implements improvements in four or five days. The improvements are usually dramatic. Each attendee makes a full-time commitment, and management empowers the team to make changes.

Thereafter, the closing cycle is improved each month by continued follow-up and improvement based on the learning and process design created in the kaizen, a perfect example of using the PDCA cycle.

CASE STUDIES

I worked with each company profiled below. Each had their own unique range of problems. Each was improved using the same kaizen approach.

Capital Equipment Manufacturer:

A single-location private company initially closed the books on an unpredictable schedule between 18-20 days. This was reduced to 5 days over a period of nine months. Then, post-implementation of an ERP system reduced it to 3 days. With further kaizen activity, this accounting team achieved regular 1-day closes for every month of the year except year-end for over six years. The key improvements included correction reduction, accuracy versus precision, and minimizing manual intervention.

Contract Manufacturer:

One of largest sites at this global enterprise of more than 50 locations was consistently late with submissions while expending significant efforts and incurring overtime. Kaizen activity resulted in a 67% reduction in processing time and a 95% reduction in wait time. The closing process was dramatically reduced, and all overtime was eliminated. The site became the benchmark for "best in class" and catalyzed significant change across the entire company.

Building Materials Manufacturer:

A single-location, private equity-owned company reduced the closing calendar from 10 days to 5 days with just one kaizen event and eventually to 3 days. The key improvements were establishing the use of standard work, coordination of efforts by team members, and the elimination on non-value add steps during the closing window.

Capital Equipment Manufacturer:
This division of a multi-division company was able to reduce the time-to-close for the cost accounting function by 50% with one kaizen event. The main improvements included gaining voice of the customer (VOC) input, reducing non-value add reports, and eliminating redundant recordkeeping and correction.

Packaging Materials Manufacturer:
A company with over 50 locations reduced the time required for corporate reporting which freed up the plant controllers to provide plant analysis and consulting. During one kaizen event, over 11,000 touch points per year were eliminated (reports x locations x frequency). Key improvements included voice of the customer, eliminating redundant reports, and creating standard work instructions. Implementation across all locations took less than 3 months.

Electronics Manufacturer (Software and Hardware):
This global company reduced their close cycle by 50% (10 days to 5 days). The initial kaizen event resulted in the identification of 223 hours/month of non-value add work to be removed from the close process as well as 124 hours/month to be removed from the close window. In addition, 21 non-value add processes were identified for elimination as part of the monthly close. A follow-on event to address the international business is expected to result in another reduction in the close from 5 to 2 days.

CUSTOMER VALUE FIRST

With Lean thinking, the needs and values of the customer are always put at the forefront of improvement efforts. As with many internal processes, not only does the external customer who buys your company's product or service not know of the close process, if they did, they really wouldn't care about it. You could have the most perfect close process in the history of the entire world, and external customers would not make decisions to buy your products and services on that basis.

So, who is the customer of the "books"? Who cares about it? And, what do they want? Answering these questions is the starting point for improving the close process. Often the customer for the close is the management team, the Board of Directors, the bank (as debt holders), and SEC analysts. To begin to improve the close and make it more valuable, you need to understand what is needed by your customer.

Below are some important questions to answer as you start the close kaizen improvement events.

1. How frequently does your customer need to see the information?

   - Are the full audited-level results needed every month? Would quarterly or annually be often enough?

   - Is some information needed weekly or daily?

2. How soon after the end of the month (or period) is the information needed?

3. If the information were available sooner, is there other reporting (early looks, estimates) that could be eliminated?

4. What is the level of precision required? This may vary by customer.

- If the information was off by $1,000, $10,000, $50,000, $100,000, would it change your decisions? The more precise the information needs to be, the more expensive in time it is to achieve.

- These decisions should not be made by the individual doing the work, but by the customer because the individual will nearly always work to a level of precision that is too high and takes unneeded and wasteful time and effort.

- The level of precision needed is typically highest near the point of action such as the depth of a cut in assembly, and lowest for those distant from the point of action such as a report to high level managers.

5. What information is strategic?

- If there is some information that makes a strategic difference to your company's success, ensure that that information is prominently available. For instance, the price and use of a precious metal might be more strategic than the price and cost of corrugated packaging even if more packaging is utilized.

- Non-strategic information should never hold up the time to close.

This line of questioning is going to result in some answers and process changes that will shake the ground under some accounting team members who have been working hard for a long time to produce data that is as perfect as possible.

This is because it was a work of art and very time consuming to get even base accuracy before computers and electronic spreadsheets. So, when everything went electronic, accounting professionals continued their prior mindset only now they were quickly arriving at and passing the precision needed by decision makers. This POV has been handed down most places to this day.

And, now with Lean, you're going to suggest that less precision is often the best way, and, yes, there will be resistance, and, yes, someone with authority may have to explain why.

Here's an example.

I was coaching and facilitating at a private company that prints and publishes materials. The President participated in a close the books kaizen event. During the mapping of the close process, it became obvious that one element delaying the close was receiving employee expense report information to match to the credit card bill.

While the President agreed that it is important to get the information, he was able to clearly say that getting the overall results quickly was far more important.

This kind of clarity was necessary to overcome the reluctance from the employee who was trying to do the job "right."

Changing not only particular steps in a process, but also the overall mindset of the work force is an ongoing challenge for every company during their Lean journey.

PROCESS MAP

After gaining an understanding of the needs of your customer, it is time to get your stickie note pads out, assemble your process team, find a big blank wall, and create a process map of the close process.

Keep in mind, that Lean events are not departmental, but complete process events. Only the people actually doing the work can present the detail required to improve the process. People involved with closing the books include all the people that provide inputs for the close including accounts payable, invoicing, cash applications, fixed assets, payroll, tax management, etc. The process map and overall event must include all the people involved with the close process whether they are inside or outside the accounting function. A couple of your customers would also be beneficial.

While there are many ways to build a process map, I have found the swim lane process map method works the best (Figure 12).

The swim lane method in general means that vertically along the left side, a name stickie is placed for each person involved with the close process. Then horizontally to the right of each name, a stickie is put up for each step that person does (the swim lanes). Next, label the points where the steps for more than one person sync up.

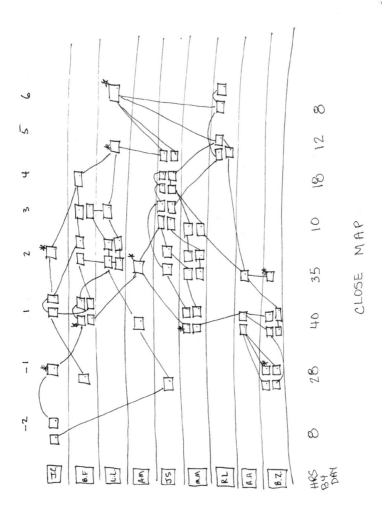

Figure 12 Swim Lane Process Map

There are a number of detailed publications on how to do swim lane process mapping.

I have had great success with the method below, and it is particularly revealing for understanding the close process.

1. Have each person put each task they do as part of the close on an individual stickie. Include (1) a short description of the task and (2) approximately how long it takes to do the work of the task (not the waiting time, just the work time)

2. Put up a tall, wide sheet of paper on the wall and mark off the days of the close. Start with close minus 2 days up through the number of days to close and do all reporting. For example, you might have 2 days before + 13 days to close + 2 days for reporting = 17 day segments on your map.

3. Have each person put up all of their "task" sticky notes. Each should be positioned on the day they do the work and in the normal order the work is done.

4. Next, draw a line from each stickie of any task that needs to be done before or after another task. Each stickie will have at least one input and/or output. These "dependency" lines make it visually easier to determine who is waiting on what from whom and for how long.

5. Next add up the number of hours of "close" work for each person for each day, and place that sum at the bottom of each day column.

6. Draw a star next to tasks that frequently have to be redone or corrected (waste).

At this point, you should have a very nice view of the current state of the close process.

CRITICAL PATH

You can take your process map a step farther and identify the critical path. The critical path is the sequence of work that if done with no lag time determines the overall minimum time required to close the books. In other words, that sequence takes more time than any other sequence. It isn't necessarily the longest sequence on a given day, because of wait times and re-do's. But without waiting and re-do, the critical path is the most time-consuming path.

Note that an absolute critical path that might be done by a project manager can take lots of analysis and time, but this method will get you close, provide valuable information, and is easily done quickly as part of a process map build.

Usually you can find the critical path on a process map of this type by working backward from the end point. On the first step backwards, look for the end input (there might be more than one) that takes the most time to complete. This is the first backup step on your critical path. From that task, repeat backward for each input or set of inputs all the way to the start of the process map.

Once you have a good idea of what the critical path is, create a document that lists the critical path tasks in order. Include who does each task and an estimate of how long it takes them.

Given all your estimates when building the process map, the odds are very high that your critical path will need some adjustments. So, use this document to verify your critical path assumptions at the next close. Put it on a clip board with some blank sheets, so it can be passed from person to person like a baton. Have each person write down their name, the task, and their start time.

Each person should start their task as soon as they get the clip board to keep the work flowing. This data will help you adjust the critical path. Remember to change the document accordingly.

As you make improvements going forward, the critical path probably will change. How will you know? By rerunning the clipboard baton verification. If the clipboard arrives at a task before the preliminary work arrives for the task to be completed, you'll know that the critical path has shifted.

This clipboard is a visual management tool and helps the team visualize the movement and flow of the close. Eventually, you will eliminate so many wasted steps and saved so much time that the clipboard will no longer be very useful!

CLUES TO POTENTIAL IMPROVEMENTS

Now that you have the process map, begin to look for tasks to improve. Some clues to look for:

- Work that does not support what customers value.

- Work that results in higher precision than is valuable.

- Overloading of work on a person on a particular day.

- Tasks that have many rework actions.

- Information that is available late.

- Tasks that take a long time.

- Tasks that are done during the close but could be done at other times or less frequently.

- Work that could be started sooner.

- Work on the critical path that has waiting time.

PROCESS IMPROVEMENTS

There are typically many wasteful, unnecessary, and/or duplicate actions discovered in a close the books process improvement event. Things just build up over time and become inefficient in spite of everyone's good faith efforts. Some can be eliminated or improved during your first event. Some can be given as homework to someone to improve after the event. Others will be discovered in subsequent events as the process changes. Do try to make all significant improvements as soon as possible.

While a given company can be an exception to the rule, below are five changes that usually can be made to the close process to reduce lead time or work time without reducing the quality of the information.

Move the close of the accounts payable "window" to the last day of the month (or sooner). This is probably the most common opportunity, has the most immediate impact on the close time, and is very easy to implement.

The open A/P window is the period after the end of the month where if an invoice arrives for the prior month, it will be entered back into the information for the prior month.

It is important to understand the amount of work added to keep the window open. First, each invoice must be reviewed to see what month it is for. This results in sorting. It stops the normal flow of work. Those days require special work procedures. Also, it means that the date for the accounts payable transaction has to be manually adjusted back to a prior month. All this can also result in many frantic errors. Don't be surprised to find that the accounts payable team leaves the A/P window open for 2-5 days. The duration is a little less frequent for public companies, as they know they cannot afford the time to leave the window open and meet SEC expectations for announcing earnings. Plus, they have found that it is immaterial!

If accountants are asked why they keep the window open, the answer will be, "It is more accurate." OK.

So, how do you get both the accuracy desired and close the A/P window before the end of the month?

A common method, especially for private companies, is to estimate a partial month of expenses at a high level with enough definition to separate expenses that are above gross margin from expenses below gross margin. Book this transaction in January. Then at the end of January, just book invoices from that day so you will have a month's worth of transactions in days. The expenses will be partial because some of the invoices will not be in yet. Invoices received in February, are entered in February, those received in March, in March. Continue this all year. In December, reverse your January accrual invoice and leave the December window open a few days to book all the years expenses. Then re-book your accrual in January. Voila!

Move entries out of the closing window. You can start with estimates. These include inventory reserve, reserve for doubtful accounts, accrued payroll, and tax reserve. Reserves are all estimates or outright guesses for amounts that will only be known precisely in the future. Therefore, find ways to estimate the reserve balances on either less than full-month information or skew the month value to a period that is off the month end.

On reserve for doubtful accounts for instance, rather than waiting to see the actual accounts receivable balance at the end of the month, use the accounts receivable balance at the end of the third week of the month.

For the accrued payroll, use a recent seven calendar days

hourly records to estimate the outstanding payroll.

The tax reserve is a huge improvement opportunity in some larger companies. One company was waiting every month to close the books for the tax department to come up with an updated tax reserve and tax rate. This rate was not used for anything except for internal books and, then, only by corporate. It was determined that corporate only needed a rate to get them into a material range. And, the only time the rate was needed for customer purposes was quarterly (if you consider a stockholder a customer), and, even then, only to a material level. This company had not looked at the close as a process and had not realized this huge waste of time and effort.

Recurring entries include prepaid accounts, depreciation, amortization, etc. These transactions are not estimates, but they can be entered far in advance of the month in which they will show up on the income statement.

Creating these entries during the close will increase the close lead time and divert accounting time and effort way from more time-sensitive tasks. If possible, pre-setup all future month journal entries, and check that they are correct once. This is very possible for prepaids. For depreciation and amortization, you may want to set up all entries for the year, and only add in monthly or quarterly additions for new transactions (purchase or sales of assets) within the year.

Do the review of invoicing, costing, and receipts daily or weekly leaving very few items to review at the close. You will be increasing the frequency of the task, but the batch size is much smaller making the research and analysis much quicker.

Further, errors are found much sooner so they do not proliferate throughout the reporting. For instance, if there is a unit of measure error on items received, you can fix this before it leaks into accounts payable, inventory work in process, or even finished goods.

Additionally, errors from problems with reference data setup, such as the Bill of Materials, Parts Master File, Customer Master File, or Supplier Master File, can be corrected very quickly so that further transactions are not errors as well.

Correcting errors very early at the source will reduce errors and waste through the system.

Move reconciliations outside of the closing window. Start with the accounts that have the fewest issues, and then resolve the sources of reconciliation issues so that they are all out of the window.

For more complicated reconciliations, consider reviewing the data more frequently throughout the month so that issues do not pile up. Another method would be to do the reconciliation less frequently; perhaps only quarterly. Another option would be to pick a day other than the end of the month to reconcile for that month.

This will dramatically reduce the amount of internal processing, sorting, and adjusting—all pure waste—you do on reconciliations. And, you will cut however long your window is out of the number of days to close!

And not to be forgotten, as with all the suggestions in this book and in *Real Numbers*, these activities comply with GAAP and can be acceptable to audited financials.

Create some minimums for relevancy for taking corrective action. For instance, what is the minimum size entry you will make to move a balance from one account to another? What is the minimum for a cross charge? What is a minimum level of reconciliation for writing off differences?

Often an individual doing a job, has a personal preference for very small minimums, but the company does not need that level of precision. Additional time for precision below the minimum is waste and could be diverted to a faster lead time or other tasks.

CORRECTING ENTRIES

Correcting entries is one of the biggest reasons companies don't close the books quickly, but they take longer and are more work to identify and implement than the process improvements already described.

A correcting entry is any entry done because the original transaction has to be adjusted in some manner. So, any splitting of entries, and moving from one account to another, any changes in the amounts, and additions of notes or account codes.

In the chapter "Using Financial Information to find Defects Upstream," the benefit of using the correcting entries (as well as other defects found in the financial information) as a way to drive upstream improvement is discussed at length.

But it is worth mentioning in this chapter about the close, because the close is when many of these errors are found. Begin to count how many correcting entries are required each month. This can be a great Key Performance Indicator (KPI) for your accounting team. The goal should be to work this number down by working with your operational partners to find ways to do mistake proofing (poke yoke) or training to avoid these errors happening again.

As you begin to capture the correcting entries, track them by $$ value. For instance, entries less than $200, from $200 to $500, from $500 to $2000, over $2000. If your company is like many, you will find the majority are in the small dollar category.

Ask yourself, "Do I want my accounting personnel to spend

time correcting small, immaterial transactions over and over. Or, do I want them to work with operations to avoid them in the first place, and not just once, but forever going forward?"

Orest Fiume, my co-author of *Real Numbers*, shared his experience with correcting entries. "In analyzing correcting journal entries, we discovered that the vast majority were for reclassification of expenses. We went through the 5 Whys, and the root cause was an overly complex chart of accounts. We did a kaizen on it and when deciding what was needed to support the Plain English P&L, we reduced the number of accounts by two thirds. A simple chart of accounts reduced the number of reclassification entries to almost zero."

A graph of the number of correcting entries by month (Figure 13) might be a very good top-level metric for your accounting team's metric board to help drive your Lean improvement efforts.

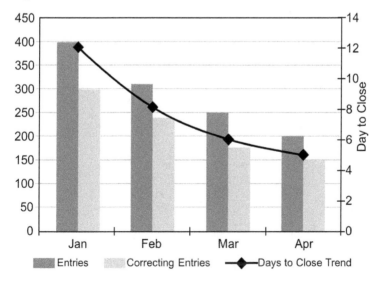

Figure 13 Manual and Correcting Entries

SUMMARY

The Value Add Accountant knows the financial statements are a required product of the accounting department. Using all 8 Wastes mentioned in the prior chapter as a lens to view your work, will yield significant targets for improvement. Just because you and your group have done a task a certain way in the past is no reason to necessarily keep using the same methods in the future.

Wasting your information and your time is too valuable to ignore. Diving deep into improving the close process will enable your group to produce more timely information.

It will also free up some of your group's time to support the demands from your internal customers to assist them in higher value business partnership work. This is the real opportunity in the future for Value Add Accountants.

5

Options for Lean Management Accounting Statements

The depth and/or existence of value streams determine how and to what degree you can implement Lean management accounting.

Early in my time as CFO at Lantech, as the organization grew to understand the concepts of flow, the company completely changed the organization structure to match the product flow. This resulted in a realignment of resources into what is today called "value streams." For each product line, Lantech created a direct functional linkage starting at customer demand, winding through the delivery of product/service, and continuing to fulfill every future customer need.

Aligning resources specifically to the product flow caused employees to be less aligned by functional work and much more aligned by the type of product and service for which the work was done. The result was a large time savings and overall simplification throughout the company thanks to far less handoff, work planning, and rework.

Resources were then aligned by product cost which made it easy to see what costs were directly attributed to different product line categories. I had been studying and participating in the Lean changes from the start and realized I could now move to a full implementation of product line financial statements without using standard cost accounting. Costs would much more easily and—more importantly—accurately be attributed to the product lines. As revenues and costs changed in the various product areas, it was easy to see the impact on the financial outcome of that product family. I knew I was starting to go against tried and true accounting practice, but my concern was to provide the most beneficial information possible to the company decision makers (while not breaking any laws or going against GAAP).

This, in turn, was the harbinger for our accounting group to orchestrate a full transformation to Lean financial statements. While Lantech was never run by financial reports, Lean financial statements made the statement information more understandable, and, thereby, more useful and valuable to the recipients, accounting's internal customers. Some, who had essentially ignored the statement as gobbledygook in the past, began using the monthly statement data such that it became an essential part of their planning and decisions. It was much easier for the accounting team to create, and operations didn't have to spend time collecting data that had never been used or understood in the past anyway.

Even my monthly employee financial presentation actually became an interesting, highly participatory session.

This shift took place at Lantech and a few other evolving

Lean companies starting in the early 90's. With the communication of it through speeches, conferences, and Lean consultants since, there is now an entire body of work in companies, education, and literature called "Lean Accounting." While Lean Accounting today encompasses much more than just financial statement changes related to traditional standard cost accounting, this early change based on Lean principles was an initial catalyst for establishing the field of Lean Accounting in study and action.

LEAN ACCOUNTING IN THE NON-VALUE STREAM ENVIRONMENT

Today, many companies worldwide have moved to value streams with spectacular results, but what if a company has not taken the steps to re-organize how the work is done into value streams? What if the product is made on shared resources? What if the product is partially made in one location and then moved to another location to be completed with other products? What if the product is shipped to various separate legal entities or foreign locations for further processing or distribution? What if the work is completely performed in functional silos?

Unfortunately, these and other non-value stream structures are still very common. It is probable that these companies simply have not implemented enough elements of the Lean manufacturing revolution to understand the extremely high value impact of true flow through value streams.

Can the use of Lean financial statements be of any value to these companies?

In *Lean Thinking*, there are five all-encompassing Lean principles that the authors, James Womack and Daniel Jones, identified in all the companies that effectively implemented the concepts of the Toyota Production System, the precursor to Lean.

1. Precisely specify what customers value.

2. Identify the value stream for each product.

3. Make value flow without interruptions.

4. Let the customer pull value from the producer.

5. Pursue perfection.

Of these five principles, two and three directly address the organizational creation of value streams: identify the value stream for each product and make value flow without interruptions.

At some companies, leaders enthusiastically find many reasons to justify why those principles do not apply to them, or cannot be implemented, or require too much investment in company-wide change to adopt. Thus, they avoid the waste reduction and value add efficiencies that Lean provides.

When working in one of those companies, you might still desire to create value by making the financial reporting statements more meaningful and useful. What actions short of full value stream reporting can be taken?

The primary methods to create Lean statements are:

- Separate variable costs from fixed costs

- Separate direct costs from shared costs

- Reduce allocations

- Use easy to understand language

- Eliminate cost system process waste

These activities taken together form the basis for Lean Accounting statements. The following sections explain what parts of each method might be applied in environments that do not operate with full value streams.

In every case, the overarching goal is to provide understandable and higher value information to those trying to make plans and decisions, both small and large, that will make your company as successful as it can be.

SEPARATE VARIABLE COSTS FROM FIXED COSTS

In standard cost accounting, all fixed costs are converted to look like variable costs and this is a major reason why standard cost accounting is so detrimental.

Within a Lean financial statement, variable and fixed costs are separated on the income statement. This is advantageous because decision making using information that treats a fixed cost like a variable cost will lead to poor decisions.

Here's is how to separate them. The context for "variable" and "fixed" relates to (1) timeframe and (2) shifts in volume.

Timeframe: Typically, a fixed cost is one that does not change in the near term. A variable cost is one that varies with changes in near term volume. Any cost can be fixed or variable depending on the timeframe.

For the purpose of explaining this method, think in a timeframe from the recent past to the next 3-6 months.

Is a Cost Variable or Fixed?

In the extreme long-term timeframe, a division or an entire business can be either shuttered or invested in. In either case,

THE VALUE ADD ACCOUNTANT

these resource decisions are fixed costs that only vary because of infrequent management decisions.

Likewise, in the very short term, when you commit to buy materials, even if you have not received them, you have committed resources that cannot be rescinded.

As a result, there are no absolutes for fixed or variable definitions! But when creating the management reports, try to match the timeframe of the information with the timeframe of the common decisions.

Shifts in Volume: Refers to the volume of demand for the product or service from the customer.

Variable Costs: The near-term costs that vary based on the shift in revenue during a particular reporting period.

Variable cost examples can include inbound freight, outbound freight, materials shipped (using matching theory of accounting), discounts, allowances, and/or commissions. Other costs that might be designated variable are utilities, warranty, planned scrap, and/or supplies if they are highly influenced by manufacturing volumes.

Fixed Costs: All the costs that are not variable, and which do not change in the near-term.

Examples might include all the people and their related costs (regardless of whether they are working in manufacturing, engineering, sales, accounting, management or any other capacity), building costs, non-cash costs (e.g. depreciation and amortization), and costs related to errors such as unplanned scrap, expedite costs, or rework. (Note that fixed costs are not based on the accounting terms, "Fixed Assets," on the balance sheet.)

Variable and fixed costs can be separated on the income statement even when not using full value stream statements.

Maintain GAAP!

When creating a Lean statement, it is important to maintain GAAP so that you do not have to create the waste of several sets of books.

You will notice that the Lean Statement definitions are not related to where they appear on the Financial Statement such as above Net Sales, Cost of Goods Sold, or below Gross Margin.

But, that is not to suggest that you throw out the traditional groupings as defined by GAAP.

In the traditional environment, start by separating the elements of standard cost into three main components:

- Materials

- Labor

- Overhead

Then, on the income statement add a Variable Margin after the variable components. This isn't a big change, but it is a step forward.

Example:

Gross Sales	$200,000
Discounts	($20,000)
Allowances	($3,000)
Net Sales	$177,000
Standard Materials	$60,000
Purchase Price Variance	$500
Freight	$400
Total Variable Costs	$60,900
Variable Margin	$116,100
Variable Margin % of Gross Sales	58%
Standard Labor	$30,000
Standard Overhead	$15,000
Variances	($800)
Total Cost of Goods Sold	$105,100
Gross Margin	$71,900
Gross Margin % of Gross Sales	36%

Why is this example better? Because unlike a traditional financial statement, a reader can much more easily identify costs that vary with volume and those that vary with management decision. This aids in accessing information specific to the decision you're attempting to make.

SEPARATE DIRECT COSTS FROM SHARED COSTS

Direct costs and shared costs are both subtypes of fixed

costs. These are costs that do not vary directly with volume but do vary based on management decisions. A direct cost is a cost that is directly dedicated to a specific product group. The easiest one to describe is materials. It is the materials listed on a Bill of Material. There are many other direct costs in all types of businesses.

For example, if an insurance company has different people who sell a variety of lines of insurance, the people selling and servicing life insurance might be different from the ones selling and servicing home insurance. All those people would be considered direct costs as they have clear boundaries of support. But, the billing department that bills and collects all types of insurance for the entire company is a shared cost.

In a manufacturing company, there might be assembly that is organized by product group (direct cost), but the machine shop or the paint line might be a shared resource. Likely the receiving and shipping areas will be shared as well.

While value streams minimize shared costs, there are examples of shared costs even in the most advanced Lean companies. Though it might only be the costs of the executives themselves.

The value of separating direct costs from shared costs in a Lean financial statement is to help the user understand what types of cost might need to increase or decrease with planned changes in volume.

For instance, if an increase in demand for product group A and a decrease in product group B is anticipated, understanding the current alignment of costs in those groupings will be valuable for upcoming management decisions related to this change.

Note that the information would already be reported by value stream in a Lean company.

Here is an example using direct and shared costs:

Gross Sales	$200,000
Discounts	($20,000)
Allowances	($3,000)
Net Sales	$177,000
Materials	$60,000
Freight	$500
Scrap	$400
Total Variable Costs	$ 60,900
Variable Margin	$116,100
VM%	58%
Direct Cost to Value Stream	$25,000
Shared Cost	$20,000
Variances	($800)
Total Cost of Goods Sold	$105,100
Gross Margin	$71,900
Gross Margin % of Gross Sales	36%

This method is much harder to implement if you are not in a value stream environment, and there will be more transactions required. If using standard cost, you will need to add a number of standard cost groupings. Some companies do this by using Labor and Overhead, but generally those are not implemented based on whether a cost is direct to a product or not. For instance, usually all customer engineering is allocated based on labor hours, which is not relevant at all.

REDUCE ALLOCATIONS

Standard cost is one big allocation. Standard cost allocates cost from a functional cost grouping to a product grouping based on some arbitrary basis. Typically, the basis is labor hours at standard, but sometimes it is broken down further to work centers or based on other factors such as material cost at standard or engineering hours at standard. By reducing allocations, the users of your statement will be able to more clearly identify responsibility for a cost element versus spreading it around to a variety of costs groupings that don't get managed at all.

If you do not have value streams, can you reduce allocations? One big step would be to allocate based on actual instead of standard hours. At least then you would have one element rooted in reality. One organization I work with now assigns the shared labor cost to individual product groups based on actual labor hour data from a labor collection system.

Does this eliminate the waste of gathering the hours? No, but at least the cost moves when people move around the factory to do different products. That provides more valuable information than whatever was assumed in the standard that was set months ago, and creating hour standards has been eliminated as well. As improvements are made at the shop floor ongoing, and people no longer get assigned to specific products or elements of work, the cost is no longer placed in that product/element.

A very easy way to reduce allocations and improve product cost data is to eliminate allocating material cost to products based on a standard price. While you may still have a standard volume reflected in a BOM (which is a very good idea), the price of goods will not be stagnated at standard but will float with any new pricing at which the goods were purchased. It is possible to switch the materials to actual pricing while retaining the application of labor and overhead at standard. Typically, this means a good is received at the PO price, rather than the standard price, and released from inventory on a FIFO cost basis. This is different from actual average costing, and actually retains the cost with each batch as received on a PO.

The value of this change is that increases or decreases in price are seen in the product cost much more directly/quickly than with a standard and purchase price variance (PPV). PPV is always a batch entry and is rarely associated with a specific product grouping/product cost. The timing of PPV is not based on GAAP, and, therefore, requires capitalization and amortizing. Last of all, use of standard price allocation drives the need for excessive material price testing as part of the audit. This is dramatically reduced with actual FIFO pricing.

Even when organized by value streams, the basic question regarding how much value there is in the effort to allocate cost is, "What is the information to be used for?" If you must allocate costs (and all standard cost systems are cost allocation systems), try to match the value of having an allocated cost, to the effort to make the allocation. For instance, if you will be using the allocated cost just three times a year to compare costs to pricing, then use an allocation method that is very simple. Perhaps just an overall closing entry of a % to various product groups or value streams.

The bottom line when a company does not have value streams (1) accounting can still save some repetitive and wasteful effort by reducing allocations, and (2) the information accounting provides can be much closer to the true cost per product.

USE EASY TO UNDERSTAND LANGUAGE

The Lean Accounting income statement is often referred to as a "Plain English P&L" because it utilizes language that the recipients of the report, the internal customers, can understand regardless of position. It purposely does not use language targeted to accountants and financial analysts. The resulting advantage is information that is more likely to be valuable and useful to company decision makers. This "layman" understanding becomes even more important if you grow into a culture of complete employee engagement and respect for people during your Lean journey.

It is difficult as a trained accountant to really appreciate how undecipherable a standard statement usually is to non-accounting employees from the C-suite on down. Providing information unlikely to be understood by the recipient is not respectful! Nor does it put usable information close to the point of use even though the accounting department might think it is doing just that.

Even when your company does not have value streams, you can examine the language used in the statements to see if it is understood outside of (or even within!) the accounting department.

The best and perhaps only sure way to effectively evaluate this is to take a gemba walk, a tool in the Lean toolbox. Gemba means "the real place" in Japanese, and it means going to the location of the activity in question to see and understand problems directly.

At gemba, you could talk with report recipients to find out what their understanding of the words are, if they know where the information comes from, and if they have knowledge of how it impacts the results. This learning can be so valuable to you, both as a means to provide easier to understand language and to understand the real practical needs of your user.

As CFO, I used a fairly simple process utilizing gemba and all the accounting team members to gather information on the current state of the statement.

1. First, gather all the key reports.

2. Then, compile a list of all the key users.

3. Divide the accounting team members into teams of two.

4. Give each team a portion of the key users to interview.

5. During the interview, one person asks the user how they use each of the reports, what the words on the statements mean to them, what does it mean if a number has a bracket (or minus sign), and what information is missing. The second team member records the user's responses.

6. Lastly, the teams come back together and share their learnings on each report.

This process should provide a strong base of information about your statement to use to improve your reporting.

Where to start in simplifying the language on the income statement which generally has the greatest need for language improvement? As in the earlier section, separate Variable Costs from Fixed Costs, and divide the Cost of Goods Sold into three components: Material, Labor and Overhead.

With the variances, rather than try to split between types of causes of variation, a title such as "Labor Spending Greater or (Lesser) than Standard" is more informative than "Labor Variance." Likewise, with overhead.

Another way to make the language easier is to describe the cost in meaningful categories such as Material (from shipped BOM), People Spending, Factory Expenses, Factory Administration, Facility Costs, and Depreciation. Provide the period cost for each, and then report the cost of goods sold and variance.

Here is an Example using plain English:

Materials at Actual Price	$800,000
People Spending	$150,000
Factory Expenses	$10,000
Factory Administration	$30,000
Facility Costs	$5,000
Depreciation	$15,000
Total Spending	$12,100,000
Total Cost of Goods Sold	$12,000,000
Spending Greater (Less) than COGS	$10,000

For some business models, there can be highly strategic costs that need to be highlighted because they have a strong impact on profitability. This might be the cost of a specific component like gold or it might be utility cost or overtime. If so, you should highlight them as a separate line item and label them in "plain English."

You will probably find the need for similar improvements in the language on the balance sheet.

ELIMINATE COST SYSTEM PROCESS WASTE

Waste in your company's cost system processes is not seen by anyone externally. As with all waste, it does cost the company money in non-productive time and lower capacity. But, the waste in non-value add time spent gathering and pumping out numbers that are not desired or used is obvious to some of those in the process and to some of those receiving the information. These are the internal customers, and rest assured they are not happy about "make-work" or worthless data.

It does not matter what type of cost system you have. There are great opportunities for waste elimination in nearly all accounting areas. Start with a user gemba walk to deeply understand what information they value.

The largest waste culprit related to the cost system is the level of precision. It is usually far too precise relative to how the information is used.

The second greatest area of waste is the reworking and correction of entries and transactions. Often, the same types of rework and correcting is happening month after month with little to no effort to eliminate those defects from happening or create mistake proofing. In fact, usually the rework is considered normal and is assumed to be a necessary part of accounting.

In Lean group improvement events, two of the tools used to expose process waste in creating accounting statements are (1) Process Mapping and (2) The 8 Wastes. They can also be applied to the costing process.

Process Mapping

1. Develop a swim lane diagram to map out who does what work and in what sequence. The diagram should include what tasks are inputs for other steps and what tasks stand alone. It needs to identify all the waiting points, the

review points, and the decision trees. A well thought out diagram provides a view of the current state of the process.

2. Next identify the steps that represent the key purpose for the overall process from the perspective of the customer (not from the perspective of the accounting team.)

With this fully developed process map for the costing system, the group can then use the 8 Wastes to see where improvements can be made while still meeting the requirements of the process.

The 8 Wastes

While the 8 Wastes are found in all processes, when you look at the 8 wastes thinking of the costing system, it is a real eye opener!

Defects: Every corrected entry is a result of one or more defects.

Over Production: Creating reports or information that no one uses. Sending information to people that do not use it.

Waiting: Waiting for information to be submitted. Waiting until the end of the month to look at transaction information or providing feedback to internal customers. Waiting for reviews or approvals.

Neglect of Human Talent: Copying, rekeying information, people untrained on system capabilities, carrying large reports or boxing them up.

Transportation: Manually moving information from one system to another, taking work to a manager or supervisor for approval because standards for acceptance are not known.

Inventory: Any work that is stopped (aka work in process or WIP), too much work on one person so that some of their work is waiting, uneven distribution of tasks.

Motion: Excess keying and rekeying, movement due to poorly organized floor layout.

Excess Processing: Doing work that does not have a customer such as copying and filing. Providing a level of precision greater than is valuable to users of the information (one of the biggest accounting wastes!)

SUMMARY

An operational shift to value streams creates the best opportunity for eliminating waste in and redefining the cost and reporting systems.

Even without value streams, there are real opportunities to make dramatic improvements in clarity, productivity, and effectiveness during the creation of income statements.

Experimentation is the key when using methodologies to improve any process including financial statements. Utilizing Lean tools and methods can produce new analytical views of the business. This, in turn, can result in new insights that can lead to changes that raise the value and use of financial reports and can establish a more important role for accounting in enterprise development.

6

Using Defects to Drive Financial Gain

Revealing Opportunity in Unlikely Places

INTRODUCTION

Defects! They cost you money every day, but you can't see them, and there are literally hundreds of them littered around your company.

For one small example, look at sales orders. In many companies, some sales orders are entered with the wrong prices every day. In each instance customers send in payments that do not match the invoice amount. Then, it takes a series of actions by multiple people to get the error corrected. This is all rework, a complete non-value add waste of time. All of these actions are ongoing defects. They are directly related to each other, but most companies do not even know that defects are occurring, nor do they have the means to "connect the dots" if one of the defects should happen to come to their attention.

This is one example of the many daily defects that are hidden and go unnoticed (often for years) in nearly all companies. Each occurrence of a defect lowers the company's productivity slightly and costs a little money, and some also irritate the customer— another cost you should consider. It is important to multiply these costs over a year or longer to grasp the long-term savings available to you by identifying and eliminating unseen defects.

Lean Business Management methods and tools are highly effective in identifying hidden defects in the business processes. In turn, the defects can be eliminated using metrics, kaizen improvement events, and daily management. You can use a method to identify these issues as defects (rather than just treating them as "normal" everyday work) and implement a comprehensive and sustainable fix. If you do, you can improve the financial performance of your organization, create capacity for growth, and improve the customer experience.

Lean Business Management (or the Lean Office) is based on the principles and methods of the Toyota Production System (TPS), which is known outside of Toyota as Lean manufacturing. To address your defect problem, an essential initial step is to understand some basic Lean concepts to see how they can be leveraged outside the factory and into the business management processes.

LEAN TOOLS

There are many Lean strategies and tools. TPS provides a well-known graphic often called the "Toyota House" (Figure 14) that shows some of the most important Lean tools and helps to visualize the system.

Starting at the top, it identifies the high level, ongoing, and constant goals for perfect safety (for customers and employees), improvement in quality, reduction in cost, and reduction in delivery or lead times. These are all outcomes (or the result) of applying the strategies shown as two pillars: Just in Time and Jidoka.

Just in Time (JIT) is the strategy of doing ALL work at the rate of customer demand. Jidoka is the strategy of understanding and eliminating the root cause of all defects to drive improvement. These strategies are implemented using an ever-evolving variety of tools such as Standard Work, Visual Management, and 5S.

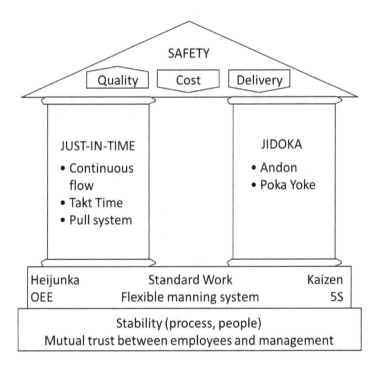

Figure 14 The Toyota House (Source: Toyota)

The base of the Toyota House has proven to be the most difficult element for many companies to address. Yet, none of the long-term gains can be achieved fully and sustained unless there is a strong base of the stability in people and processes and mutual trust between employees and management.

While most of the activity that is taught and discussed in the Lean world is the impact of JIT (lower inventories, improved lead times, on time deliveries), the enabler for this ongoing improved performance is Jidoka.

Just in Time

JIT stands for "Just in Time" and encompasses the (1) pace, (2) movement and (3) sequencing of doing work.

The pace of any process is how many are made/done at a time, how frequently the work is done, and how that work relates to demand rate.

TPS emphasizes a JIT process that strives to work as closely as possible to the rate and mix that customers demand the work, making one at a time (aka one piece flow), and keeping the work moving at all times.

Proper sequencing results in very low levels of inventory, minimal waste from producing the wrong work, and short lead times.

JIT concepts and tools should be applied to processes in the factory and the office (business management). By constantly striving for perfection in these areas, creativity and unique solutions to waste are discovered.

Jidoka

Jidoka is a Japanese word that means "automation with a human touch." There are four principles:

- Detect the abnormality

- Stop the process

- Fix or correct the immediate condition

- Investigate the root cause and install a permanent countermeasure.

Applying Jidoka means striving for quality, mistake proofing, and improving on an ongoing basis.

Lean strives for quality at the customer demand level. In other words, trying to understand the customer's needs and matching or delighting the customer.

Mistake proofing attempts to make it impossible to do the work incorrectly; whether separating manual from automated work, physical adaptations, or other means.

Improving a process is based less on a master plan and more on examining the defects that happen while work is done. Use a defect(s) to identify the next areas for improvement, understand the root cause of the defect(s), and change the process to eliminate the defect(s).

DEFECTS

The JIT and Jidoka concepts apply equally in both the factory and the office including every process in your company.

By continuously striving for perfection, through experimentation and problem solving, waste is minimized through creative and often simple solutions.

Eliminating defects or waste has always been a management goal, but hidden defects are nearly always overlooked.

Mr. Katsuaki Watanabe, a former president of Toyota once said, "Hidden problems are the ones that become serious threats eventually. If problems are revealed for everybody to see, I will feel reassured. Because once problems have been visualized, even if our people didn't notice them earlier, they will rack their brains to find solutions to them."

A long time ago, Henry Ford, a strong link in the historic management chain leading up to Lean, said, "The easiest of all wastes and the hardest to correct is the waste of time, because wasted time does not litter the floor like wasted material."

And, an icon in business management, Peter Drucker states, "There is surely nothing quite so useless as doing with great efficiency what should not be done at all."

The purpose of this chapter is to describe how you can use Lean techniques to improve your accounting team's value to your company by two wide-ranging methods.

First, how you can identify defects that are built into your daily business processes and, in particular, in your daily accounting transactional work.

And second, how you can apply Jidoka methods to leverage that information and start providing a new high value and high impact leadership role for the accounting team in process improvement across the organization.

ACCOUNTING PROCESS DEFECTS

Much of the work of the traditional accounting function has a transactional basis.

If you consider the triangles in (Figure 15), the base of the triangle is the transactional work. The next layer is analysis, and the top layer is consulting work. Analysis is making sense of the transactions; and consulting is using the analysis to help improve the decision-making and future results of the company.

Internal and external business partners want (and need) more consulting from accounting. But accounting's time is mired in the transaction. ("Transaction" refers to the ongoing work such as paying bills, collecting money, closing books, paying taxes, inventory tracking and similar).

Some accounting professionals might like to do more analysis and even consulting, but are not sure how to engage beyond the historic role of being the "accounting police." Everyone is fully busy, and it's true, you can't just stop doing this ongoing work. However, you can use Lean techniques to reduce waste and defects and dramatically—very dramatically—lower the time needed to perform transactional activities. Then you might do more consulting.

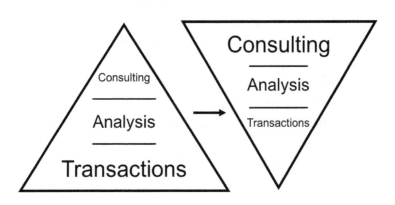

Figure 15 Accounting Work: Traditional to Lean

What enables the accounting team to see the business management defects within the transactional processes? You can dissect the work starting at the financial statement. The statements are a reporting of the aggregation of accounts. The accounts are listed in the trial balance. The accounts balances are a result of debit and credit transactions (double-sided accounting) that are made based on every business transaction that either initially or eventually will affect money!

For example, a supplier delivers goods to the company. A transaction is recorded of the receipt of the goods. This transaction will show a receipt of inventory (The debit which in this case is an asset.) and an obligation to pay the supplier (This could be accounts payable or goods received but not yet invoiced, which is a credit and, in this case, a liability.). These transactions in most modern companies are prepared as part of the information systems/enterprise resource planning (ERP).

Another very typical example comes as part of the cash receipts process. An invoice is created and sent to the customer. Accounting transactions are created with a sales transaction and an accounts receivable transaction. The customer decides— through their own flawed processes—how much to pay the company. The payment is sent to the company (or lockbox). Again, more transactions with an increase in cash and a decrease in accounts receivable.

Eventually these transactions make their way to the accounting department. Following our example of goods received, typically an invoice is sent from the supplier to the company. A person in the accounting team (usually an accounting clerk) will do some work with this invoice. For the received goods example, they may manually compare to the purchase order, or to the receiving document or transaction. Sometimes this comparison will be done manually; sometimes electronically. With the incoming cash transactions, the payment is matched to the open invoices for the customer (usually by purchase order number). But in either case, our "Eureka" moment is at hand.

If the invoice does not match the other documents, this is a defect and requires 100% non-value add rework to fix it!! Reflecting back on the Toyota Production System environment, a defect is the magic moment. It is the signal that something is wrong with the business management process! At this moment, no one knows what is wrong, or who is wrong, or how often this problem happens, but, by golly, they are going to search for root cause and fix it so it doesn't occur again.

But in the non-TPS or non-Lean environment, no one is probably thinking about any wrong or defect since this error probably recurs all the time and is considered "normal" and acceptable.

What typically happens in companies when this error (defect) is found will vary. But in most places, the focus of the activity is to fix that one instance immediately. In other words, getting the documents changed so they match, and then proceeding. Or creating a correcting accounting entry. A permanent fix is not considered because this type of rework is considered just "normal" work. But, when these types of defects are analyzed, they are often found to account for most of the transactional time in accounting.

Let's take that defect apart a bit. First, remember that the time used to process an accounting transaction initially is extremely minimal. In fact, it is often automated and takes no time at all from the accounting team. But, to correct that single defect will take many, many steps. These include setting the defect aside, going back through the issues later, emailing or contacting the key parties, waiting for them to get back, asking another round of questions, more waiting for them to get back, resending documents, and maybe some finger pointing until finally reaching agreement to proceed. One defect fixed (until the next time it occurs).

Another example of defects that can always be observed when examining the accounting information is the accurate recording of normal business activities that just didn't go the way expected. Defects all. Consider the accounts we have identified for this type of work: scrap, expedited charges, obsolete inventory, etc. And, consider the amount of work that goes on that is represented by these accounts.

Of course, not every type of defect or opportunity for improvement (The 8 Wastes) is seen in accounting transactions, but many are. What are the kinds? There really is an endless list of defects that can be identified in accounting operations. Consider these typical examples:

- Supplier invoices differences in quantity, cost or business terms

- Cash receipts that do not match the company invoice in quantity, price, or business terms

- Expediting charges for incoming or outgoing transactions

- Return material credits (ingoing or outgoing)

- Scrap transactions

- Missing transactions (not invoicing for services provided)

- Obsolete inventory

These are all considered normal and necessary errors when running a business, but they are actually defects that can be minimized or eliminated altogether saving incalculable time and effort for the company over the long term, and accounting should lead the charge in doing just that.

DEFECT METRICS

Rather than putting all your efforts for these defects into fixing each individual case, what if you could identify what types of defects happen most frequently and/or have the greatest financial impact, and, then, start minimizing or eliminating them? To do this, use the tools of metrics and decide what you want to track, how often the defect happens, and identify what are the main reasons.

First, work with the accounting team to create a list of "categories" of errors (defects) that result in rework. Examples of categories include:

- Payment did not match invoice

- Supplier invoice did not match

- Expedite charge incurred

- Inventory transaction incorrect

- Correcting entries

Select 5-10 categories from the list.

Second, at a very macro level, identify where the quantity and/or cost of each error category is seen. For example, if you want to know how many invoices do not match, your source of information would be the accounts payable clerk. If you want to see how many customer payments do not match the company invoice, you could examine that with the cash application clerk. If you want to see how much scrap there is, you could look at the trial balance.

Third, go to the source and gather the quantity or cost macro level information about each category. If you don't have the historical info, manually track it for a couple of weeks. This will probably not reveal the root cause of the errors, but will provide you enough information to decide where you want to focus your initial improvement efforts.

Fourth, analyze the macro level info you gathered, and (using the cash receipts example from earlier) assume you have and decided to focus on the defect category of a customer payment that does not match the invoice (but is unrelated to early pay discounts or other company contractual agreements).

PROBLEM-SOLVING

With your category defined, you are ready to launch a problem-solving effort. This is the point where accounting steps out of the "police" role. This is the point where accounting starts to behave like a business consultant. This is value add work that every accounting team member can participate in that will benefit the company and make them a partner in the Lean journey. This is also where you begin to actively work across traditional functional boundaries and become a partner in the company's Lean efforts. A Value Add Accountant is born.

Value Add (VA) and Non-Value Add (NVA)

Classifying work as "value add" or "non-value add" is a method to enable focus on work being performed that your customer does not want to pay for. Non-value add work is waste and a defect.

This is not an indictment of the person doing the NVA

work, it may not even be work you will decide to completely stop. But it is work that you want to look closely at to identify ways to reduce the time and cost of the work, or in many cases eliminate it altogether.

Reducing or eliminating non-value add work, increases capacity by freeing up people and resources to focus on work of greater value to the customer and organization.

Tools

The Lean tools that work very well with this type of problem solving include process metrics, process mapping, the 5 Why's, kanban, and even some 5S! There are many ways to attack understanding the problem, finding the root causes, and implementing solutions. In my experience, following these steps yield the most efficient results.

1. Gather the data.

2. Identify and segregate each reason for the defects. Select a reason.

3. Look at the data to find some themes or hints to common traits for the reason selected. Select one common trait.

4. Create a process map that identifies the overall process.

5. Get out, move, and talk.

6. Determine root cause.

7. Brainstorm at least 5 solutions.

8. Select a solution and design an experiment to see if it is effective.

9. Launch the experiment.

10. Monitor for results.

11. Adjust the experiment.

12. Create and train standard work.

13. Determine where else this solution can be applied.

14. Return to the overall data and select the next experiment.

APPLYING THE PROCESS

Using the cash receipts data as an example, this section discusses in detail how to apply the 14 steps and also provides guidance for improved utilization of accounting's business consulting role.

1. Gather the data:

Working with the cash application clerk, collect data for one or two weeks. How many invoices are paid at a different amount than the invoice?

2. Select a high occurrence reason:

Identify a few high occurrence reasons and create a "reason bucket" for each. Typical reasons are: "Different Price," "Different Quantity," "Deduction w/o Credit Memo," and "Unknown." For each invoice that does not match, place it in the correct reason bucket. Select one reason with a lot of mismatched invoices to work on.

3. Choose a common trait:

As an example, assume "Different Price" is the reason selected. Within the Different Price invoices, take an initial review of the invoices and see if you can find a common trait for the error. Possibilities include "a specific customer," "a specific sales person," "a specific type of product," or "a type of invoice" (manual versus EDI versus system generated).

Select just one high quantity trait. Include the cash applications clerk in deciding. The clerk will likely have a good idea of what the common problem trait might be. Assume for this example that you have identified the common trait as "Make-to-Stock products."

4. Create a process map:

Using the swim lane method of process mapping, create a high-level map of the "life" of one invoice for a Make-to-Stock product. Start at the beginning of the process. This is typically when the price of the item is established.

Now, list and document the high-level steps in the process up to and including when the invoice has been received by the cash applications clerk.

Process Map

A process map is a tool used in problem solving, especially in the Lean Office, to make work ("the process") that is hard to see more visible.

It visualizes the workflow on a detailed physical map, and it identifies the "who," "how," and "when" of the work being performed. The map usually crosses functional corporate boundaries.

Swim lane process mapping creates a "lane" for each person who touches the work, just like a swimming pool lane. This makes it easier to see each person who is doing work, where in the sequence each person's work is performed, and how their work relates to other steps in the process. The "Close the Books" chapter has more on processing maps.

5. Move & Talk:

And now begins the magic. Get out of your accounting department, and go talk with all the different people who are part of the process map that you have created. Ask for their help in understanding and documenting how the process really works.

Document each and every large and small step in the process. The number of steps will surprise you. Continually update the process map as you ask for help for different parts of the process. This may seem a bit tedious with the first process map, but it is essential because the map will make work (including defects) that is hard to see, observable.

If you put the map in a location where it can stay, be visible, and easily accessed by all, you and the other process members will use the map over and over as you continue process improvement activities. The map does not have to be perfect. It should change (reflecting defect/waste reduction) and be updated in a timely manner reflecting the importance of the activity.

6. Find the root cause:

With a reality-based process map in place, choose some examples of mismatched invoices for Make-to-Stock products (the defect common trait), and separately track each of them through the process map. By doing this, you will start to see where the defect occurred and how it was able to happen.

Try not to cut off this analysis too soon! Challenge the

team to ask, "Why did that happen?" five times (The 5 Whys Lean tool) or until you get a specific causative reason (the root cause) that you can take action on

A common failure point is "The person wasn't trained." But, go further than that. Why was the person not trained? Are there training materials? Is there a standard process? Is there cross-training?

On a problem like this, it is very common that you need to/should engage the external customer. Before you do that, look very closely at and thoroughly understand your own process. For example, Company A (who I have worked with) found that the reason the wrong price was paid by their customer, Company B, was because of a file with updated prices Company A sent to their purchasing department each year. The file was sent to purchasing with no preparation or follow-up to see if the update prices could also be updated into the Company B's computer system (which it turned out, was never done). Once Company A found the root cause, it was an easy solution to engage Company B and have their system updated each time the new price list was sent out.

You may find more than one root cause contributing to a defect. While it is a judgment call, try to not solve too many root causes at one time, since you will not be able to discern what solution is actually having impact.

7. Brainstorm solutions:

This is a step sometimes overlooked often resulting in less than optimum results. Once a root cause has been identified, you might feel so relieved that you grab onto the first idea that someone throws out on how to fix the problem and rush off to implement the solution. However, real magic will happen if you slow down at this point and brainstorm.

Your goal should be to address the root cause and eliminate the defect thus avoiding any reoccurrence. Force yourself
and your team to identify at least five different potential
solutions. Identify and write all five on a flip chart before you
evaluate even one of them. This takes real discipline. But, if
you can do this, you will find that you rarely pick the first solution that was proposed. When you have five (or many more)
ideas, select the 2 or 3 ideas considered best for discussion.

8. Select solution and design an experiment:

With your 2 or 3 ideas, see if you can quickly test each of
them. The first method is to go back to your current state
process map and see how the map would change if you went
with the first idea. Do this for each idea selected. Would the
idea actually work? What else would need to change

Another way to test is to take the original invoices/orders
that had problems and apply each solution. Would one or
more solve the problem? Either of these methods should
enable you to agree on a single solution

Next, create an experiment to use the solution for some
actual orders or for all orders for some period of time. The
experiment might be for a set period of time, or for a certain
type of order, or just one person or small team

Create written job instructions, samples, and what to do
in special situations. Define when the experiment will end.

If possible, do not create an experiment that requires
system change. Do it manually at first. Not every experiment
will work. You want to do it quickly and ensure it has the
impact you are expecting before creating system changes.

9. **Launch the experiment:**

It sounds simple, but this is a common failure point. When you launch, make sure each person involved understands this is an experiment. Go over the instructions. Ask for their input and suggestions. Make sure all team members know who to turn to with questions, and make sure that person is available to them.

10. **Monitor the experiment:**

During the experiment, check in with the team members at least daily to see how the change is working. What are the results? Has the defect stopped? Daily monitoring not only gives you fresh feedback and focus but also demonstrates the importance of the experiment to the team.

11. **Adjust:**

The experiment is rarely exactly right the first time. But you will know what is working and not working from feedback if team members are encouraged to take ownership

But, avoid making undisciplined adjustments to the experiment on the fly. While daily monitoring, discuss as a small team how to implement the adjustments needed. Re-establish the job instructions and samples leading up to each adjustment, so that every team member will understand how important it is to have everyone doing the work the same way so the experiment can be truly evaluated

At the end of the experiment, determine if you want to implement the change. If so, move to the next step. If not, continue the experiment and keep adjusting!

12. Create standard work:

Create the standard work, samples, and work procedures to implement across the relevant range of work. Train each of the people impacted by the change. Emphasize the need for standard work. But, also emphasize their process ownership and encourage continuous improvement ideas.

If the solution changes are small, this will be quite simple. If the changes are large, then use of training sessions, a buddy system, or other change management approaches may be needed.

13. Extend the solution:

Many solutions will improve processes beyond your initial problem. Think about other scenarios that the solution might be able to benefit. It may be another location, or a different type of order, or a different customer type. Use the power of this successful change to leverage additional process improvement.

14. Continue to monitor metrics/data and experiment:

Returning to steps 1-3, continue to monitor for defects, and select the next type of problem or the next high impact trait within the same category. Use this step-by-step problem solving for all the types of problems that you can see within the accounting processes.

Does the process above sound like more work than you are willing to take on? Think about the types of problems you work with every day. Many of these problems affect your financial results, affect your employees work life, and affect the customer experience.

The work of problem solving will allow you to implement process improvements and AVOID many of your current problems in the first place. These are problems that you have inadvertently invested in by having employees using their time to correct them for years and years. These little problems eat up the capacity of your company and do not endear you to your customers.

This metric driven, problem solving activity using Lean continuous improvement techniques should be an ongoing part of every business and every function.

By the way, no one ever gets all the defects. New types of unexpected encounters that create defects occur continuously throughout every business every day. But, every defect you permanently solve adds a little available capacity for your company for every time that defect won't occur in the future, and with Lean you can solve many, many defects.

SUMMARY

Occasionally a CEO will decree "Lean" as the new order of the day, with an entire strategy for learning and implementing. But, many companies have to start small perhaps just in their department. By starting small, you can practice and learn Lean improvement methods and "spread the word" so others buy into the methodology. The momentum of change will not only help your company grow, but enable it to grow more productively.

A transformation occurs from hiding errors, grousing about errors, and finger pointing to "revealing problems" and "racking our brains" to find a solution. Each improvement saves time, increases capacity, and ultimately favorably impacts the bottom line. This is the key to Lean Business Management.

What if there are 10 improvements? 1000? More? Each

one providing its small gain every time the defect does not occur forever.

And the accounting team discussed in this chapter? They can become a key resource in helping to guide the path for continuous improvement. Accounting reports and results affect management and decisions throughout your company.

As accounting consultants (with their newly available capacity due to reduced rework time needed), they can participate in improvement events elsewhere in the company and lend their expertise to improve and speed up the improvement events of other functions. As with IT, accounting's presence and knowledge in improvement events usually improves the event when questions of numbers, reporting, and systems come up as they often do. The resulting higher visibility will cause accounting to be included in a wider range of decisions throughout the company as well.

As has happened in many Lean companies, accounting becomes more a partner and less the "police," employees gain a broader company knowledge, have a more interesting diverse job, and mutual respect and understanding between functions often follows.

There are a lot of win-wins in the Lean corporation.

7

Materials:
Big Cost; Little Attention

For many manufacturing companies, the largest single cost is the cost of the materials that are purchased to build the products. And yet, it receives by far the least attention in the presentation of financial statements. Often, it receives the least attention from the accounting team as well!

Real Numbers opened the issue of target costing. This chapter discusses the importance of accounting engagement in product development.

MANAGEMENT AND FINANCIAL STATEMENTS

Starting from the outside moving inward, how easy is it to see the material cost of your products?

External Statement Cost format: Normally it is impossible to see the material component.

The format is:

- Net Sales

- Product Costs

- Gross Margin

- Gross Margin %

No cost of materials visible there. In fact, it is hidden completely.

Management Statement: It starts to get a bit more interesting. The decisions of how to report product cost internally is under the control of accounting as long as it is in compliance of GAAP or IFRS. The materials cost will be reported between Net Sales and Gross Margin. But many ways to report exist.

One of the typical layouts show:

- Net Sales

- Cost of Goods Sold (COGS at Standard)

- Purchase Price Variance

- Labor and Overhead Variances

- Other variances

- Other manufacturing costs

- Gross Margin

In this case, we can guess that materials are in the COGS and perhaps some additional material pieces in the Purchase Price Variance, and in some of the other variances. But you need to be a detective and have a very good friend in cost accounting to figure it out, because all the product costs are merged together and then applied to the products losing identity of cost type.

Sometimes there is more detail:

- Net Sales

- Materials at Standard

- Labor at Standard

- Overhead at Standard

- Materials Quantity Variance

- Purchase Price Variance

- Labor Variance

- Overhead Variance

- More variances

- More manufacturing costs

- Gross Margin

In this case we are getting a bit closer to see the materials in the products, adding together several lines.

Lean statement: you will normally see Materials content completely separated for the other product costs:

- Net Sales

- Material Cost

- Other Variable Costs

- Variable Margin

- Manufacturing Period Costs

- Adjustment to Labor/Overhead in Inventory

- Gross Margin

In this case we can see the Materials Cost.

But even here, all the materials costs are reported as one number.

Consider how different that is to the other product costs which are broken down into very specific areas such as wages, salaries, overtime, benefits, scrap, supplies, etc. Or, costs are separated into department types such as welding, assembly, plant management, customer engineering, quality, purchasing, receiving, etc.

And yet, the biggest cost on the income statement is just one number, "Materials." Are there different types of materials? Of course, including steel, components, adhesives, packaging, purchased items, etc. Or, they could be separated by purpose such as motors, coverings, power supply, packaging, and more.

Even most ERP systems only have one account for the materials without any specific opportunities to break it down. Additional fields within the part master field are used to identify type of part, but information is rarely (if ever!) used to assign the material cost to a separate account in the chart of accounts.

VALUE ADD AND NON-VALUE ADD THINKING

An important Lean concept is Value Add (VA). There are three criteria used to evaluate if something is Value add.

- It transforms materials or information

- The customer is willing to pay for it (i.e. it has a purpose to the customer)

- It is done right the first time

If work does not meet that criteria, it is considered Non-Value Add (NVA).

But what is the PURPOSE of determining if work or activity is Value Add? Is it important to know how to classify? No, though classification is necessary. The purpose is to guide your focus and reveal all the existing non-value add activities (waste) so you can analyze and brainstorm improvements. It's to enable you to reduce the time and resources spent on non-value add activities. It's to lead you to see how to do the work right the first time. It's to cause you to find a way to eliminate the task. It's to get you to think about how to reduce the time and effort to do the task. It's to show you that there is waste in your process, so you can find a way to reduce or eliminate it.

Waste reduction is the core principle of continuous improvement and Lean thinking, and separating every process element into value add and non-value add is how you start of find the waste.

MATERIAL COST AND VALUE ADD

Can VA/NVA thinking be applied to a material cost? All costs are the results of both quantity and price.

- Sales $ =   Quantity x Price

- Material $ =   Quantity x Price

- Labor $ =   Quantity x Price

- O/H $ =   Quantity x Price

You can evaluate Material Cost based on the cost of its two components: Quantity and Price (Figure 16).

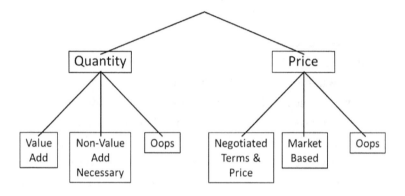

Figure 16 The Cost of Quantity and Price

Then you can look at each component, and evaluate that component based on Value Add, Non-Value Add but Necessary, and Non-Value Add and Unnecessary.

Material Quantity

- Value Add Material: Customer uses these materials in the intended function of the product

- Non-Value Add Necessary: Materials utilized if the production process works as designed, but the customer does not utilize during the use of the product

- Non-Value Add Unnecessary (Oops!): Materials used when the process is not performed to standard.

Material Price

- Value Add Price: Price that has been negotiated with the supplier considering the full set of terms, quality, and customer rate of demand.

- Non-Value Add Necessary: Pricing based on market conditions not influenced by purchaser

- Non-Value Add Unnecessary (Oops!): Extra cost in price for expediting, unnecessary packaging, incorrect price on invoice/purchase order, etc.

Once you have evaluated each component, you can decide what you should do with it. Figure 17 shows how you would typically want to address each result.

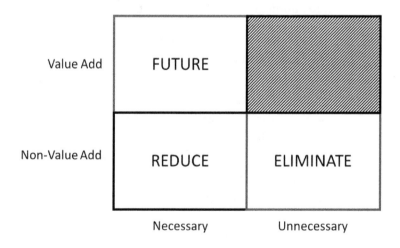

Figure 17 Value Add vs Non-Value Add

EXAMPLE

Here's a detailed example for quantity using a white board marker (Figure 18).

- **Value Add Quantity**: Customer uses these materials in the intended function of the product. Examples might include:

  » Ink used in function of the marker over its lifetime

  » Barrel used to hold the marker

  » Felt used to carry the ink

  » Cap used to keep the ink dry

- **Non-Value Add Necessary:** Materials used when the process works as designed, but the customer does not utilize during the use of the product.

  » Ink not used in the function of its lifetime

  » Extra felt in the barrel beyond requirement

  » Carton

  » Case

  » If .5% are tested and then thrown out, the materials in those units

  » Ink washed out of the equipment during changeovers

  » Solvents used to clean equipment during changeover

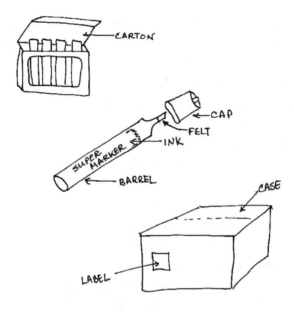

Figure 18 Materials for Manufacturing White Board Markers

- **Non-Value Add Unnecessary (Oops!):** Materials used when the process is not performed to standard.

  » Materials scrapped due to defects or mistakes during manufacturing
  » Materials purchased but not used

PARTNERING ON MATERIALS AND PRODUCT PROFIT PLANNING

Most accounting effort looks backward. It ensures materials are paid for properly, reflected in the balance sheet, and recorded when not utilized properly.

But where is the effort to work for the future towards the

quantity and price of materials that will be used in new products? Where are the high value decisions to determine the very best materials being done?

Is it on the shop floor? No, manufacturing has no influence of the material cost. They produce based on a bill of materials. They can influence scrap cost but little else.

Purchasing also has limited control. They can help find an optimal price and terms by shopping with suppliers. And, this can have a beneficial effect in time. However, the material specification is not within their control.

It is usually entirely in the product development stage that all the material parameters including the quality, quantity and specification are determined.

If your company has adopted Lean 3P thinking (Production Preparation Process), each of these areas, Product Development, Purchasing, and Operations, are brought together. Then, they collectively use their expertise to optimize the cost and revenue profile of new products. 3P is a huge step forward in optimization and waste reduction for companies using it.

But for accounting purposes, the questions are, "What is the role of the accountant in the decisions related to the product cost and revenue profile?" and "Who is doing the high value work to determine the right materials from an overall financial perspective?"

As with other matters, you will find most members of accounting focused on backward-looking activities related to materials. But, there are a few accounting teams I have worked with that assign resources to work closely with product development in product planning activities. For that is where the most important profit decisions are made for the future.

Typically, if financial analysts are assigned to product

development or the R&D team at all, they are only there to monitor the spending of the function and not to focus on the profit generating outcomes of the function. This is an opportunity lost for accounting, product development, and the company.

How can you and your accounting team begin to change this gap in engagement with product development?

The easiest first step is to assign an accounting person, like yourself, to attend new product development team activities. This might be just regular attendance at the daily or weekly stand-up huddle. It might be to attend the product development staff meeting on a weekly or monthly basis. If there are new product design or introduction teams, ask to join the team and attend on a regular basis.

Initially your presence will raise a few questions as nearly any change does. Allow yourself to just be in the moment, listen, and learn what kinds of topics are discussed. Listen for the connection points of their conversation and the impact it will have on material selection and specification. Look for connection points to revenue opportunities. Do not be surprised if you begin to be asked to help with understanding as it relates to costs, assets, and the impact of various decisions.

You may not have those answers, but you have the language of accounting. They do not have the language of accounting and need support connecting the dots from the decisions they make to the impact on financial performance.

For instance, they may not understand:

- How cost is reported for tools or dies differently than the cost of materials in the product.

- How to think about large volume purchases for small quantity utilization.

- The difference in evaluating the cost of work that requires hands-on labor versus work done by CNC equipment programming.

Being present, listening, learning, and providing assistance where needed can be the starting point of a new kind of partnership that can benefit future profitability.

OPTIMIZE MATERIAL PLANNING PROACTIVELY

For a more active and advanced approach, establish a team representing the key functions. Team members would include:

- Product development engineer

- Product manager

- Production leader

- Production worker

- Buyer

- Product User (or representative such as Sales)

- Cost analyst

Select a specific product and gather key information about the materials. A BOM is a good starting point, as well as any scrap, warranty, inventory, and buying information available.

For each element of the BOM, determine volumes purchased and then how those volumes are utilized between value add, non-value add but necessary, and Oops.

Each team member would bring their experience with the

product. Establish the current state. A spreadsheet of the information—using the white board marker example—might look
like Table 2.

Item	Part No.	Quantity Purchased	Price $	Cost K$	VA	NVA Nec	Oops	VA K$	NVA Nec K$	Oops K$
Felt	FX3847	350000	0.023	8,050	9500	339500	1000	218	7,808	23
Plastic Pellet	3433	470000	0.015	7,050	257000	113000	100000	3,855	1,695	1,500
Ink	All	7800	0.35	2,730	50%	40%	10%	1,365	1,092	273
Carton	All	4000	0.18	720		95%	5%	-	684	36
Case	All	300	2.3	690		95%	5%	-	655	34
							Total K$	5,438	11,935	1,866
							%age	28%	62%	10%

Table 2 VA vs NVA Product Analysis

With this established as the Current State, jointly establish targets and improvement opportunities.

MATERIALS KEY PERFORMANCE INDICATORS

An important and costly oversight when material planning is the responsibility for materials metrics and key performance indicators (KPIs). Consider the following four materials-related metrics:

- **Material Cost as a % of Sales:**
  Almost entirely based on product design (both the materials cost and the sales price. But, who is responsible for the metric? Is it the Product Development?

- **Scrap as a % of Sales (Anticipated):**
  (or % of Product Cost/Material Cost) This is often considered as materials yield buried deep in the standard or product cost. Manufacturing has no control on this, but Product Development and Purchasing together can manage this cost. If it is significant in the cost, who is addressing the drivers of this cost?

- **Scrap as a % of Sales (Unanticipated):**
  (or % of Product Cost/Material Cost) This is typically the cost of materials that need to be scrapped due to an error or mistake. Manufacturing has primary control of this factor.

- **Obsolescence or Slow-Moving Material Reserve as a % of Product Cost (or Material Cost):**
  The estimate of cost is the joint responsibility of Product Development (specifying materials that can only be purchased in large batches), Purchasing (buying large

quantities to get a per unit price break), Sales (providing inflated estimates of demand), and Scheduling (planning the manufacture of the product in advance of customer demand). Who has the metrics for this cost?

When accounting focuses on the materials content of the products, it is performing a higher value consulting activity as a business partner with Operations and increasing future profit and customer value.

SUMMARY

More than elsewhere in this book, this chapter highlights the need for the accountant to become an active part of determining the course of the company's future.

For companies that produce products, materials are typically the largest cost element. Material decisions are significantly affected only during development activities. Yet during development, materials get little expert cost analysis, and material cost overall is usually poorly understood.

As the accounting team reduces effort needed to perform normal accounting transactions, they will have available capacity to engage beyond their traditional role.

So, engage with product and service development. You have the analysis expertise to interpret immediate and long-term product costs. This is a very high, value add opportunity and even a responsibility when applied during the development cycle.

Do it! And, become an active, valuable participant in development activities that will determine the future profit and success for your company's products and services.

SECTION III

Go Take Action

8

Getting Started

Lean Accounting is more than making one or two improvements and saying, "We are doing Lean." or "We are now a Lean company." It requires (1) ongoing interest and observation, (2) belief in waste reduction as critical to achieving best results, and (3) pointed insistence on building continuous improvement thinking as a primary driver in managing and leading your business.

Every bit of waste reduction is a positive, but most companies that casually practice Lean leave a vast amount of opportunity unrealized.

So, if Lean focus is not a leadership style currently established in your function and/or company, how can you get started?

GO SEE SOME LEAN

If your organization is using Lean in other functional areas but not accounting, an easy starting point is to have some of the accounting team members visit Lean activities in other parts of the company.

Attend a weekly or daily huddle or improvement session.

Attend a presentation for a kaizen or improvement event. Invite members from other functions to come talk to the accounting team about what Lean is in their area. A highly impactful activity is to participate in a kaizen event for a process that you may or may not be part of directly. Every kaizen event needs participants who are not "inside the box" of the process being improved.

As team members visit other areas, devise a process where they report what they saw and heard to the other accounting team members.

GROUP READING AND RESEARCH

When the accounting team feels they are prepared to start their Lean journey, there any number of options for initial learning.

Many teams start by creating a reading group. They select a book, perhaps one on Lean Accounting like this one, and then read one or two chapters a week with a scheduled, 15-minute group discussion on what they learned. Some like to do this at lunch in a leisurely atmosphere where distractions of the job don't interfere. If reading an entire book is too intimidating, you could ask for a volunteer to read one chapter and report out. Then, rotate with others reading subsequent chapters.

I don't provide a reading list because Lean books are being published so rapidly, and a list would become dated quickly. I suggest searching on "lean accounting books" specifically or "lean books" to see a wider list.

Another option is to identify online resources that have recorded content that team members can watch and discuss.

For Lean Accounting articles, blogs, videos, etc. in general, search on "lean accounting." I suggest not just looking at the first page list. Some of the best resources are often further down the list.

LEAN TRANSFORMATION COMPONENTS

There are three main action components in a Lean transformation: Strategic Deployment, Managing for Daily Improvement (MDI), and Value Stream (or Process) Management (Figure 19). Value Add Accountants strive to engage at all three levels.

Strategic deployment activities are those motivated by executive direction and are intended to dramatically "bend" the future outcomes of the company for the better.

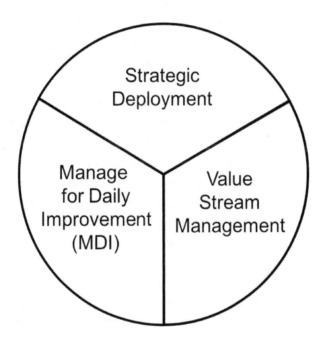

Figure 19 Lean Transformation Components

Managing for Daily Improvement focuses on self-driven enhancements within a specific team or group. Improvements are based on process improvement and waste elimination. Some will be individual improvements. All group members participate. All improvements, large and small, are important. They are made ongoing, announced publicly within the group, and acknowledged by management.

Value stream management includes improvements that cut through the organization with multi-functional engagement focused on driving customer value.

STRATEGIC DEPLOYMENT

For Lean to become more than an occasional improvement tool in your company, a top down focus must be developed with the goal of creating a continuous improvement (CI) culture. This is hard work and will take years of concerted effort to become sustainable both at the functional level and top management level.

Company leadership, C suite members and other top managers, must let all company members know they value time spent on waste reduction using Lean principles and tools. Initially this can be shown by including Lean waste reduction in the strategic objectives, scheduling Lean introductory classes, and discussing Lean at company gatherings, departmental meetings, etc.

Then, the leaders have to back it up by their actions. Employees know a leader's true priorities from their actions. Words are important, but actions over time are reality and will drive employees to focus on their waste reduction efforts (or not).

This means leaders must not only verbally endorse activities but participate in them as well, and ask follow-up questions concerning the improvements a few days, weeks, or months later.

In accounting, this leadership role falls to the CFO, VP of Finance, or, in small companies, the Controller. An enthusiastic, knowledgeable employee can use Lean techniques for individual work or within a process, and can influence the CFO to get involved, but leadership must initially carry the torch and rekindle the torch periodically in order to pursue, establish, and maintain and overall CI culture.

THE LEAN CFO

In accounting's world, it is ideal if the CFO can set the stage by articulating that "improvement" is real and valuable work. There are many ways to do this including:

- Making "Improvement" and agenda item at every staff meeting.

- Assuring people who are attending improvement activities that they are not expected to be in two places at one time (i.e. being scheduled to be in other meetings or activities.)

- Providing for cross-coverage and some leeway in deliverables...especially at the beginning when improvements have not yet freed up significant capacity of the team.

If the CFO is not available to provide this overarching expectation, then it can also be provided by the local finance leaders. Leadership needs to promote and discuss the culture of CI to gain momentum. As improvements start, it is important to talk about improvement activity and share support and recognition for those involved. It's also important food for thought for those yet to be involved.

Recognition should go to every improvement whether it is a single saved step an individual thought up or a thousand "touches" eliminated by a kaizen event team.

As CFO of a single location team, I started my staff meetings by asking, "What has been improved since we last met?" I set an accounting team goal of getting at least 52 improvements each year. Each improvement, whether great or small, counted as "1." The staff kept count and discussed their progress at each meeting. I called this "Q52" and it is discussed in detail in *Real Numbers*.

For a time, they were focused on reducing the close the books cycle. I found having the staff meeting after the close each month was a good time to reflect on their improvement progress and the issues they discovered as part of the close. They tracked the number of manual and correcting entries and brainstormed ways to lower the number the next month.

The accounting team celebrated at the end of the year if they got at least 52 improvements. In 13 years, they celebrated every single year! It makes work even more enjoyable when there is fun and pride involved.

For a CFO at a multiple location or business unit team, such intimacy might not be practical. As an example, one CFO—at a client I consulted with—had 55 plants. He fully supported Lean improvement efforts but had to rely on his local accounting leaders at each site to drive the improvement effort. To lend the weight of his position to the effort, he personally recognized one plant each month for improvements implemented and asked that location to share their benefits. The company created a traveling award for recognition…just to have some fun and treat people with respect.

PURSUING LEAN WITHIN ACCOUNTING

What if your CFO is not interested in pursuing Lean improvements or moving toward Lean Accounting? That's where the enthusiastic, knowledgeable employee mentioned earlier, the developing Value Add Accountant, will have to start individually or with a small team, and, then, with some concrete success, expand and grow the effort over time.

Not that you should make the effort without informing your

superiors. Make the case, get the okay, and then start.

The first step on your journey to Lean Accounting should be to communicate that there is real interest in looking at how work is done and encouraging experiments to make changes. Not just change to what "other people" do, but change to what you and your group do. Display a willingness to consider different approaches and share ideas within the accounting team.

Improvement activity will need to be positioned as real work; not "extra work." When it is seen as extra work, then no one will ever have the time. No one has ever had extra time in any company or in any function!

MANAGING FOR DAILY IMPROVEMENT

The simplest way to begin your Lean Accounting journey is to create a time for making improvements within the team focusing on accounting work the team does.

Managing for Daily Improvement (MDI) is a structure you define that legitimizes and advocates for work time and effort to make changes.

MDI can be done many different ways. Back in the 90's, I created the Q52 structure mentioned earlier. It worked great and is still recommended.

However, as Lean moved more and more beyond manufacturing, many started borrowing ideas from the production based SQDC huddle, and today the "huddle" is widely used as a starting point for establishing Lean waste reduction throughout many companies. Many of my clients use huddles with great long-term success.

THE HUDDLE BOARD

The structure of a huddle reflects many elements that should be included in any MDI activity.

1. There is a set time and location to talk about improvement progress.

2. The number of improvements made will be tracked. This provides feedback and it is easy to see if the effort lapses. It should also be used as a rallying moment for celebration.

3. A huddle is typically weekly and lasts no more than 10-15 minutes. There are many processes that thrive with daily huddles as well. The huddle is not where problems are solved. It is where focus, discussion of potential improvements, selection of which improvements to address, and monitoring cadence occurs.

4. Employees own the huddle. Company and functional leadership provides support and encouragement.

5. With a mature huddle process, there is a board listing metrics, communication, and a skills matrix. Also, backlog, in-process, and completed improvements are listed.

One of the easiest ways to create your first huddle, is to put up a simple improvement flow board using stickie notes that are easily moved around (Figure 20). The board is used to display ideas on possible improvements or specific waste targets.

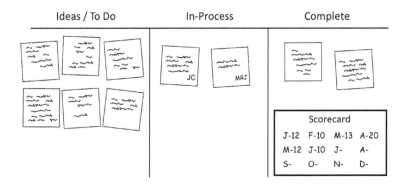

Figure 20 Improvement Flow Board

The huddle members use the board to decide which ideas to work on, and as appropriate, they move chosen ideas to the In-Process column and add the name or initials of the person leading the effort. Completed improvements move to the Complete column.

During the huddle each week, the person chosen to lead the effort gives an update and moves completed ideas to the Complete column when done.

When any accounting team member makes an improvement within the normal scope of their work, it can be added to the Complete column even if the idea did not move through the board "flow."

At the end of the month, add up the number of improvements completed that month and write it on the score card.

This is a really simple description of how it works, but simple is a really good way to start. It keeps the initial focus on the joy of improvement and not on the hassle of procedure.

As time goes on, you will find what procedurally works well for your group.

HUDDLE GUIDELINES

You will make changes to your huddle process as your group learns by doing.

I have noticed that for those who have a daily huddle, it is best to rotate the leadership role weekly. And with a weekly huddle, rotate it monthly.

If you are only doing a monthly huddle, try to do the huddle more frequently. A shorter interval will drive more activity and improvement, maintain focus, and build more camaraderie in your team.

As your huddles matures, you might want to create a topical script for the huddle. A script establishes a common procedure for the huddle and makes it much easier to rotate the leadership of the huddle each week or month.

A script (standard work) for a very basic huddle might be something like this:

1. Welcome to our weekly huddle. (10 seconds)

2. Did anyone complete an improvement this week to add to the board? (1-3 minutes)

3. Let's get an update on the in-process improvements? (4-8 minutes)

   • Ask each improvement owner, one by one, to give an update of 2 minutes or less.

   • If the improvement is complete, move it to the Complete section.

4. Are there any improvements to start this week? (2 minutes) For each start, ask who would like to lead it and add their initials to the sticky?

5. Are there any new improvement ideas to add to the board? (2 minutes) Have each person with an idea write it on a sticky and place the sticky on the board before or during meeting

6. If it is the end of the month, add up the number of completed ideas/stickies, and put the number on the monthly scoreboard.

7. Thank you! (10 sec)

Here are some other suggestions to help your huddles go well:

- Set a time limit for the huddle of 15 min or less. Have a timekeeper, and if it gets to 15 minutes, stop the huddle. Start where you left off at the next huddle. (Pace and flow)

- Do not use the huddle to solve the problems. It is only to get updates and decide on which new improvements to start.

- Break down improvements into small bits that can be completed in two weeks or less.

- Avoid using the huddle for large initiatives. Huddles are for the daily improvement activities (Larger, more complex, or time-consuming improvements should be raised to the kaizen event or strategic level.)

- Anyone who is the leader for a current in-process improvement, should not lead another in-process improvement at the same time. (one piece flow)

- A report out about results and improvements should be by team members and not by the huddle leader. (Engagement)

- Keep track of the number of improvements. (Metric)

- Every 4th meeting, spend 5 minutes discussing how to make the huddle better. (PDCA)

YOUR HUDDLE EVOLUTION

The huddle process and board can include many other enhancements. And, you might want to enhance yours once the basic structure is established, understood, and used effectively by the accounting team.

There are many possible enhancements. Your unique business environment will govern the enhancements you adopt.

Visual information is an important component of every Lean company, and the huddle board is a perfect visual medium to add associated information for everyone to see and use (Figure 21).

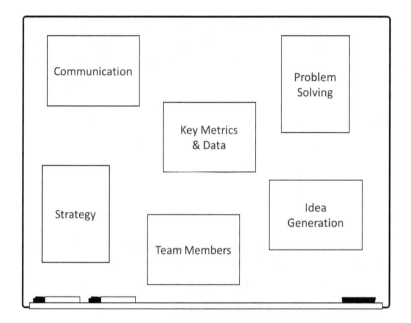

Figure 21 MDI/Huddle Board

Some information teams have added to the board include:

1. Calendar of upcoming events/targets

2. Metrics or Box Score

3. Status of larger initiatives

4. Skills matrix and assessment

5. Attendance at the huddle

6. Overall company outcome metrics

7. Key information and workflows

8. Pictures and names of team members

It is most common that the board a group starts with is NOT the board they use for the long term. The visual board aspect combined with the huddle meetings will engage and motivate the workforce to focus more on eliminating waste. Once a group sees this, they will add other complementary information to the board to increase its use and value.

So, when you start, avoid fancy expensive materials. Use sticky notes, flip chart paper, markers, etc. Then it is easy to change and adapt.

HUDDLE RISK

The greatest risk to the improvement value of your huddle is when a group starts using the huddle as a means for discussing current work and upcoming tasks, and not spending the time on MDI process improvement.

This can happen early on when the huddle environment is not well established or later and especially when group leadership changes.

Your huddle board metric showing the number of completed improvements may be your best indicator to see if your group is staying true to the MDI objective.

In an attempt to avoid this, some will emphasize the "rules," by posting them. Here's a good example.

MDI Focus on Continuous Improvement

Role of Manager

1. Provide regular, stable time, and location for huddle.

2. Allow time for CI work by all employees.

3. Encourage improvements and experiments.

4. Ask questions about barriers. Ask if employees need help.

5. Step in only on issues that employees have not been able to solve themselves.

6. Verbally reinforce that CI is "real work."

Tips for Success

1. Huddles: 15 minutes or less, CI focus, preferably once a week (at least, every two weeks).

2. Let employees lead the huddle.

3. The huddle is not where problems are solved.

4. Only one problem or improvement at a time for any one person; don't overload.

5. At least 1/2 of problems/improvements are within the team versus for a separate team.

6. Keep track of the number of improvements as the primary measure.

VALUE STREAM MANAGEMENT AND PROCESS IMPROVEMENTS

Once MDI starts and people are on the lookout for waste elimination targets, you will undoubtedly find wastes that negatively effects accounting processes but do not seem to be generated by accounting. Thereby, you'll need involvement from upstream or downstream groups to eliminate those wastes in accounting and overall.

This might be the point that you decide you want to completely reassess how you get work done; especially the work that crosses functional boundaries. This is Lean Thinking starting to build momentum.

Many if not most processes in your company cross departmental and functional boundaries. You and other members of accounting need inputs from other functions and perhaps even from external sources to complete your work. You, in turn, provide output to other functions and areas. All of these inputs and outputs are part of your accounting processes.

The essence of Lean Thinking is to deeply understand what customers, whether internal or external, need and to focus your efforts on meeting those needs with as little waste as possible.

Customers do not care how your company or group is functionally organized. They do, however, receive the benefits from the passing of work through your functions. The passing of this work is a process. The customer often receives benefit from processes they may not know exist.

For instance, the customer may not care about how you get materials and pay for them, but they know you must have materials for their products (even if they buy services from you!). Or, they may not care how you file your tax returns, but they do want to work with suppliers who can stay in business and have a quality reputation.

Most processes stretch across functions and include handoffs from and to people in wide ranging departments. Thereby, the work to improve the process necessarily must include all the participants of the process. And, everyone has to let go of traditional department and functional barriers to do this.

This is often difficult and foreign, but luckily Lean methodology provides tools to break down these barriers for the purposes of waste elimination. These tools are (1) kaizen improvement events and (2) process mapping.

THE KAIZEN EVENT

What is a kaizen event? In its purest form, it is a cross-functional improvement activity.

For instance, if the kaizen event is focused on a process such as setting up a new customer, it might include involvement from the sales, order entry and credit functions.

Or, the kaizen event could focus on a value stream such as a specific product line or a specific customer type. In that case, it would include the involvement of many functions who deliver value to that specific value stream.

Entire books have dealt with how to have great kaizen events.

I have planned and facilitated countless kaizen events in Lean Accounting and otherwise. While the basic structure of an event is straight forward, the details for some functions including accounting can be unique and must be understood by the facilitator.

Kaizen = Change for good

To help you get started with this indispensable tool, below is a condensed view of the typical sequence for a typical kaizen event.

A kaizen event has:

- 10-18 cross-functional members: some upstream in the process, some downstream, some who do the core work, and some who are not even in the process!

- Attendees who attend the event full time. They do not dash in and out after checking email or messages or show up when they get around to it. This is necessary for continuity and to give the event a sense of priority and value for all attendees. Others might be included periodically in the role of subject matter experts.

- Attendees who are cross-hierarchical and potentially from any level of the company. And, they all—that means every-body including C-suite members who participate—put their titles aside as an equal member of the kaizen event team.

- A team that is empowered to make changes in the process.

- A dedicated and, preferably, contiguous time schedule. For an accounting event, the best events tend to be 3-4 days. That is enough time to really complete each activity and immediately implement some improvements.

- A set sequence of activities that is followed.
  1. Event purpose and definition with scope and objectives.
  2. Some basic Lean training.
  3. Map and understand the current state. This is the most important activity.
  4. Define and create a future state map.
  5. Brainstorm and select improvements to the process.
  6. Implement improvements. This is second most important activity and should require 50% or more of the time of the kaizen event.

7. Assign homework. Some improvements will not be able to be implemented during the kaizen timeframe. Assign homework to a team member for each one. The team member follows up and manages the implementation of the improvement and reports the results back to the team.
8. Document and share the results.

To optimize improvements, use the 8 Wastes and value add Lean methods to identify which current process steps can be eliminated, moved, or changed. This often includes changing who does the work, how frequently the work is done, or sometimes even adding more work!

Do not focus your kaizen event on information system (IS) improvements. IS should not drive the change. It is the last thing to change AFTER the changes to the actual process have been designed, tested, and agreed on.

IS professionals, who probably know little about the inner workings of your accounting process, might well try to lock your process into what they think is best for the system. But, what is best for the system is often not what is the most efficient and valuable way to redesign and execute your process for accounting and your company.

Not focusing on the potential IS improvements is very hard for office workers. IS focus is a real pitfall of Lean Accounting and other process improvements because it reduces experimentation and significantly slows the rate of improvement.

This is not to say that you should never improve the system. You should, but only to match the IS up with your now optimized process. If the information system is your first target of improvement, you will be disappointed with your results over time.

PROCESS MAPPING

Many Lean thought leaders including myself are huge fans of processing mapping for business transaction work. It's amazing the amount of hidden process waste mapping finds.

When I first participated in kaizen events, it was in manufacturing. They didn't use process mapping. Instead they simply went and watched the work happening on the manufacturing floor (Gemba Walk) in order to learn about the current state.

But when I later steered my groups (e.g. accounting, HR, IT, etc.) to (1) go beyond the physical nature of materials transformation (manufacturing!) and (2) start to look at the processes that transform information (almost everything else!), going and looking was still beneficial, but it wasn't enough to capture in detail what work was happening.

What to do? We started utilizing the Lean process map tool. It helped kaizen event teams dramatically to hear and see how work flowed in the process.

I found the swim lane process map style worked best. It lists each person or job that is part of the process, and it displays the sequence in which a given "unit" of work passes through the process. It also allows for any potential permutations to be added in. Swim lanes are discussed thoroughly in the Process Map section of the "Close the Books" chapter.

The purpose of the process map is to help the kaizen event team to learn and understand the current state. Going in, no one will understand the details of the current state. A few may think they do at the start, but that will not last.

The map is developed with stickies on large paper sheets taped to a wall. This makes it visual to all. It's easy for anyone in the group to reference it, ask questions about it, question its correctness, offer suggestions, change it, and overall, better learn about the process.

The process map does not have to be perfect. But, it needs to be close because the entire kaizen team needs to understand the work being done and how the current process works. In turn, that will enable them to best evaluate how to change the process to do the work better in the future.

PICK A PROCESS

There are so many processes in accounting and finance. Some of the processes accounting has primary responsibility for are listed below. All have numerous opportunities for improvement.

Finance/Accounting Services

- Payroll
- Forecasting/budgeting
- Treasury
- Audit
- Decision Support
- Cost accounting
- Inventory management
- Closing the books
- Management reports
- Accounts payable
- Credit
- Collections
- Capital assets

Deciding which process to start with might be difficult. Here are three approaches that might help you decide.

- Biggest pain area: Generally recognized as a problem area by people doing the work or by customers of the work.

- Many people involved: Many people doing similar work whether inside or outside accounting

- An opportune learning process: A process fairly well known by many that makes it easy to work cross-functionally (especially if working cross-functionally is new for your organization).

In my experience as both CFO and consultant, I've found the two processes easiest to start with are "Close the Books" and "Accounts Payable." Chapter 4 of this book addresses Close the Books in detail.

For Accounts Payable, it really isn't "just" Accounts Payable. Accounts Payable is part of the larger process of compensating vendors for materials and services provided to the company. It may also be viewed even broader to include identification of suppliers, procurement, and through compensation.

But as one of your first kaizen event processes and to maximize your ability to understand and conduct kaizen events, scoping your initial accounts payable process a bit narrower will be helpful.

In planning a kaizen event, you should start with a scope statement and objectives. The example below includes a sample scope and objectives for accounts payable.

Scope

Topic: Paying Vendors for Goods & Service

Starting Point: Invoice received from vendor

Ending Point: Payment sent to vendor

Exclusions: Payroll, letters of credit, international
shipments

Inclusions: Invoices with and without purchase orders

Objectives

- Reduce the number of invoices requiring rework from 30% to 10%

- Reduce missed discounts from $1500 to $750 monthly

- Reduce touch points by 25%

- Make 10-15 improvements

- Learn about Lean and have fun!

As you can see, it is fairly simple to create and very open ended. The scope and objectives can be modified by the team to make sense for your company. You can use this general format to establish a scope and objective regardless of the process you select.

What you do not want in the scope and objectives is a solution. If you already have solutions that you have decided to implement, don't create a sham engagement activity as a kaizen event. You may well destroy the credibility of kaizen events in general for your group.

However, if you've thought of some possibilities for a solution, a kaizen event may be an excellent means to evaluate those as well as ideas from others as part of the event steps. At the end of the kaizen your ideas will have been verified or another, better idea will have come to light. A waste reduction win for everyone regardless.

SUMMARY

You must take action.

Getting started is only your first step to becoming a Value Add Accountant. Each step thereafter leads to more and more learning and waste reduction.

It won't be perfect. It will be messy.

But change is required to eliminate the large amount of hidden waste currently in your processes. Every organization is ever changing, and each change might well introduce additional waste within the interconnected processes.

If you are in a company that has started its Lean journey in production or elsewhere, the changes will be better orchestrated but more rapid. Regardless, accounting will be impacted and starting your Lean journey today will help you support your changing organization.

Adopting Lean principles will also raise the respect for and utilization of the genius that all your company members have, but much of which is often latent in command and control environments. That genius can be released using Lean tools to improve accounting processes and organizational outcomes.

9

Communicate Lean Improvements

Seeing is believing. Just telling people about the potential of something is often not enough to get them to actually change their behavior. So, it is with Lean.

An important, early step in the Lean transformation is building momentum during your first Lean experiences. Teaching and using Lean tools with your people are initial activities, but the journey will not gain any momentum without people understanding that Lean improvement changes will yield better results that benefit everyone up and down the organizational hierarchy.

You will need to find ways to PULL people toward Lean thinking.

Art Byrne, former CEO of The Wiremold Corporation, and author of *The Lean Turnaround*, shares his perspective of how to create "zealotry": Start with executive leaders demonstrating the importance of improvement, second commit to kaizen events, and share successes.

LEAN PROMOTION

This is not easy. Think of the work of promotion as parallel to the work to get a large boulder rolling. At first it takes a lot of effort. But as more and more people join in and more hands are pushing, the boulder starts to roll. As the momentum increases, the boulder gets easier and easier to keep rolling. This is the same with Lean efforts. It may start slow, but through communication of activity and results, others join in, the effort gets easier, and, eventually, you're rolling.

In general, few organizations take promotion of programs through sharing and reinforcing seriously. This in spite of most leaders knowing that the more profoundly an idea is embraced, the more pervasive is the change and benefit to the organization.

My Lean experience has shown over and over that the best way to pull people in and create some Lean zealotry, is to (1) publicly share the actual improvement successes that you have and (2) have executive leadership demonstrate and reinforce that improvement work is important and expected. It must be valued as real work, not just "when we have time."

But, can this be done with decrees and broad platitudes? Probably not. Jumping on the business authority's bandwagon because "he said so" hasn't worked to promote enthusiastic and sustainable change for quite a while in most places.

You will certainly need to communicate your Lean improvement commitment and goals at the start, but you will also have to "sell" Lean ongoing by including it within many of your other business activities.

The purpose of this chapter is to provide you a few ideas to consider on how you can do that.

HUDDLES

There are lots of communication opportunities if you are holding daily or weekly huddles.

The huddle itself is a visual indicator. People within visual range who see co-workers standing up around a huddle/communication board tells them there is enough interest in the culture of improvement that some are willing to spend valuable time doing something about it.

Create a schedule for every employee to visit huddles in other departments so they can see how huddles work and to generate new ideas for their group.

Invite people from other huddles to attend your huddle. This adds a level of seriousness that helps team members realize this is an important component of your management system.

Occasionally (or monthly) hold a joint huddle with other teams to share the improvements from each team. An example is scheduling the accounting team and the IT team to have a joint huddle.

SHOW RESULTS & METRICS

If you publicly display improvement activity and results, those involved will thrust their chest out with pride and many of those not involved will wonder why they aren't part of the action and might want to get onboard.

Identify a very public location. More than one location adds legitimacy. Create displays for improvement activity to be added to, posted, and celebrated.

- Improvement opportunities.

- Current improvement activities.

- Improvements implemented.

Similarly, you could post A3's in progress and completed in a common area.

Create before and after images of activities. They say, "A picture is worth a thousand words.," and improvement activities provide many ways to visualize the improvement experience.

- Photos of physical changes.

- Diagrams.

- Before and after process step maps.

- Changes to report layouts.

- Photos of team members engaged with improvement activities.

Be sure to post metrics in the work place. People are either interested in them or awed by them. Both reactions help. Regularly update them and describe the improvement actions taken.

Create a graph that shows the number of improvements being made on a weekly or monthly basis with a goal line. For instance, if you goal is 52 improvements in a year, provide a line graph that displays cumulative progress toward that goal (Figure 22).

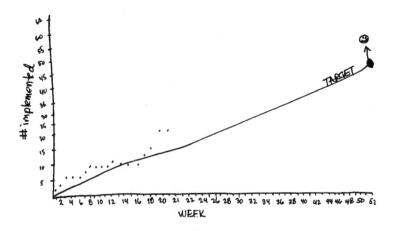

Figure 22 Improvements Implemented

One group monitored the time between improvements as a way to show the pace of improvement (Figure 23).

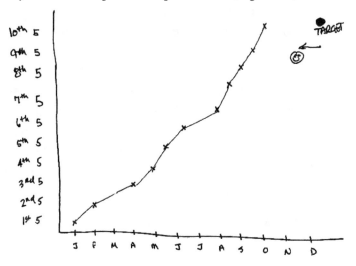

Figure 23 Pace of Improvement

IMPROVEMENT EVENT PRESENTATION

It is critical that every kaizen event should have a report out presentation to company leaders. Participants include employees of the process affected, management, and executives. Participants should be encouraged and thanked for their learnings.

Management should celebrate and recognize the team efforts. They should ask what was this like? Would you want to do again? What did you learn? What do you need from management to be successful? At this celebratory time, management should NOT put people on the spot and ask about why the solution was selected or what the impact will be.

A broader, more visible improvement presentation can be very powerful for all employees. Try this. Define a set day and time each week for presentations of all kaizen events or other improvement initiatives to report the results though visuals. The presenters should be actual event participants if possible. If high level decision makers consistently attend these presentations, it sends a very strong message about the importance of improvement.

Two large hospitals I worked with have this type of event. In one case, the public is invited to attend. In both cases, the CEO attends and, as a result, the executive staffs as well.

This clearly demonstrates that the leader is creating an environment that is expecting improvement work to be done.

The presentation should be very short using standard work for the presentation. Consider the following topics.

- Current state.

- Future state.

- Improvements implemented.

- Means to monitor.

- Impact. (Each improvement team member presents or talks about how it affected them.)

COMPANY MEETING, C-SUITE RECOGNITION

When a C-suite member talks, most everyone listens.

Regularly scheduled company meetings should have a standard agenda item to discuss improvements made to the processes and recognition for those—especially non-manager employees—who have made outstanding improvement contributions.

I had a client with over 50 locations. The CFO could not visit every location regularly, so he had a monthly call with all the divisional controllers. During the call, the CFO recognized a location and the improvements they made. The location also received a traveling plaque to recognize their efforts. Logistically, the corporate finance Lean leader made the selection of which location and improvements to recognize, but the recognition was given by the CFO at the monthly call, and he led the subsequent improvement discussion.

GEMBA WALKS

Management and Lean experts should be doing gemba walks—going to where the work happens—ongoing for their own Lean learning and to praise others for their improvement efforts. This is common in manufacturing areas, but it is also important to understand accounting and other office related events. Changes and results may not always be physical, but there is always something to show electronically or with a sketch at a minimum.

Leaders should be asking questions during every walk. How much time will this save your group? How has this improved the process?

A leader feigning interest will soon be discovered and become a grating negative. But, the interested, enthusiastic question will break down workplace barriers, and the information flow can be thrilling for everyone.

Ask a lot of questions. What other improvement ideas do you have? Who was most effected by the improvement? Are you planning any other events? Did this improve or hurt your work day? Do you think there is more to improve?

People love to tell what they know and experience.

NEWSLETTER ARTICLES

If you have a company or accounting newsletter, use it as a vehicle to "advertise" and praise your improvement activities.

- Create a regular feature with a catchy name such as "Culture of Continuous Improvement."

- Post interviews of people who have been part of Lean activities

- Include a schedule of upcoming kaizen improvement events or other Lean activities.

- Post guest improvement articles written by your Lean champions, managers, or anyone who has an improvement story to tell.

As your Lean improvement efforts accelerate an entire improvement-oriented newsletter might be successful.

ACCOUNTING TEAM MEETING

Do you have a regular accounting team meeting? If so, use it to show the importance of improvement. (If not, you might consider one for many leadership reasons!)

At the start of each accounting team meeting, ask what has been improved since last meeting. This demonstrates by the leader that the work is important, and that it is the work of the employees.

Initially, you might have to nicely encourage participation by asking questions, but once your group hears you throwing out praise for improvement a few times, they will start coming prepared to tell everyone about their improvement.

You might even create a simple award—chocolate usually works nicely—to throw out after each improvement declaration.

WEBSITE

Create a simple internal website or collaborative SharePoint type site where people can post their improvements and share stories. Provide functions to add comments, share, tag, etc. The online discussions that can ensue from this type of site can help everyone to learn about and devise more improvement suggestions.

References to these stories by executives and leaders can go a long way in legitimizing Lean efforts in the eyes of employees.

PUBLIC SHARING

As you become more deeply engaged with Lean thinking, consider providing opportunities for others outside the company to learn from your efforts.

Be a host location for a group like AME[8], MEP[9], LEI[10], etc. and offer public workshops in your conference area. Be sure to take the participants on a tour and highlight the "before and after" of your improvements.

Create a time once a quarter where external people can sign up to get a formalized tour where employees share their successes and challenges.

Contact your local newspaper and encourage them to do an article about your Lean improvement efforts.

Schedule an open house to share your Lean efforts with other companies.

These are not just ways to "show off" what you have achieved. While it may well raise your company's standing with the participants, it might also firmly communicate to your employees the importance and impact of their improvement actions.

COMMUNICATE TO THE BUSINESS WORLD

Many magazines are interested in case studies and will provide a reporter to create the story. These articles can also be a great way to communicate across the organization that Lean is an important and valued part of the culture.

There are conferences put on by accounting and/or Lean organizations for training and communication best practices. Someone on your team could volunteer to present at one of these forums. Many conferences are very eager to have companies present their story for others to learn from. If the session is recorded/taped, make the recording available within your company to show those involved with improvement—hopefully, everyone—that they are helping to promote your company to the outside world.

SUMMARY

Nelson Mandela said, "A leader is like a shepherd. He stays behind the flock, letting the most nimble go out ahead, whereupon the others follow, not realizing that all along they are being directed from behind."

To get some followers after you have created an environment for the nimble to go out ahead, you need to share what others have done. Sharing accomplishes several goals:

- It communicates that other people inside the company have begun to act.

- It provides improvement examples that will generate ideas by others of what they might change in their areas and processes.

- It demonstrates that management values this work.

- It provides contact points for those ready to jump in.

There are many, many ways to communicate. The best solutions for your company will be determined by you and others who value and promote Lean improvement. However, solutions will not invent themselves, and they cannot be successful without upper management participation.

Start thinking now about how a Lean communication plan can work in your group and in your company.

10

Convince the CEO/CFO to Adopt Lean

What if the company you work in is not involved with Lean or perhaps there are just pockets of Lean activity sprinkled around the organization?

There is much written about the importance of leadership by the CEO in creating a change in strategy and culture.[11,12] My experience strongly supports this perspective and suggests that the role of the CFO has a huge impact as well on the success of achieving superior outcomes from adopting Lean and an overall improvement strategy.

When the CEO and CFO clearly and consistently demonstrate their commitment to improvement through words and—especially—deeds, the organization will notice. In turn, improvement efforts will get higher prioritization and have far greater results.

The opposite holds true as well. When the CEO and CFO are not actively promoting the improvement culture (whether through Lean concepts or other improvement-based concepts), the entire organization will quickly ascertain that the effort to manage and support change is not important.

What can the accountant do to create desire by the CFO or others within the company to investigate Lean and turn to an improvement and customer focus? The good news is that you can present the CFO with a strong financial case for Lean as you have read in earlier chapters. The Lean revolution really began because MIT researchers were interested not only in Toyota's consistent high quality but also in their incredible market value when compared to their competitors.

WHY DO LEAN?

No company has to do Lean, but those who don't risk being left in the dust by one or more or their competitors who are.

There are abundant reasons why a large and growing number of worldwide manufacturers have adopted Lean principles. Leaders today in a wide range of industries, nonprofit organizations, government agencies, healthcare, and other areas are applying Lean principles. They see it as the best method available to produce goods and deliver services that create value for the customer with the minimum amount of waste and the maximum degree of quality.

Further, the early 2000s assumptions by many that, "Lean is only for manufacturing." has been impressively buried by successes in innovative companies in nearly every industry.

Stories abound concerning the dramatic, unexpected gains in shipments per employee, lower inventory, and better delivery times when manufacturing initially adopts Lean principles. Just as important or, perhaps, more so from a long-term impact perspective, are the ongoing gains not only in operations but in other areas as Lean principles are applied to departments and functions throughout a company. My observations from my Lean clients and from the wide range of industries represented at non-manufacturing Lean conferences I attend demonstrate this accelerating shift. Outside of production, Lean application is often called the Lean Office or the Lean Business Management.

Lean is an indispensable competitive advantage worldwide that puts non-practitioners at competitive risk. Lean applies to any size company and to any size process. High profile practitioners include FedEx, Alcoa, Dell, Intel, United Airlines, Kimberley-Clark, Parker Hannifin, Caterpillar, Nike, Boeing and on and on. Following the Lean success by individual members, entire industries such as healthcare and construction are producing white papers and creating industry learning groups on Lean principles and practices.

ELIMINATE WASTE

All of the gains produced by applying Lean ultimately come down to the elimination of waste.

Presumably, most companies minimize obvious waste within their business processes, but Lean principles comprise a dramatic, enterprise-wide change in assumptions, concepts, values, and practices that collectively reveal very large and expensive areas of hidden waste within a company. As practitioners who have implemented Lean beyond manufacturing will confirm, Lean principles and tools can and should be applied to all business processes.

As you might predict, this fundamental change is not easy or completed overnight. Lean adoption cannot make your company a star overnight, and your company is not "Lean" because someone ran a kaizen event last Tuesday. It usually takes 5 years or more of concentrated effort with top management focus for a self-sustaining Lean environment to be created.

However, this long-term effort is not a reason to avoid Lean because (1) one or more of your competitors is probably already gaining from Lean, and (2) with the very first improvement event, unexpected and often dramatic gains do occur. Each event will eliminate waste and lower some combination of time required, space needed, rework, employee frustration, material usage, etc. Your employees who participate in Lean events will see this improvement. That will lend obvious, concrete support to your early Lean efforts and help everyone to "get on board."

Importantly, the methods used to implement Lean principles are proven, well documented, and can be easily understood by everyone from the CEO to the line worker. An internet search of any Lean term returns countless links and Lean literature abounds. Some Lean principle terms have even worked their way into the business lexicon including kaizen, one piece flow, sensei, kanban, pull scheduling, and JIT.

THE TOYOTA PRODUCTION SYSTEM

Lean principles are fully based on the Toyota Production System (TPS) developed over a 30-year period after World War II and widely shared by Toyota starting in the early 1990s.

Toyota's goal was to provide best quality, lowest cost, and shortest lead time through the elimination of waste. Toyota's success is well known, and their products and methods revolutionized the automotive industry over the past 30 years.

And financially, Toyota's market value in the automotive industry has simply been off the charts for a long time.

Rank	1950	1970	2001 Units Sold		Mkt Cap (4/2002, $B)
1	GM	GM	GM	(8.30)	34
2	Ford	Ford	Ford	(6.90)	27
3	Chrysler	Chrysler	Toyota	(5.93)	101
4	Studebaker	VW	VW	(5.11)	18
5	Nash	Fiat	Renault/Nissan	(4.98)	14
6	Kaiser –Fra.	Toyota	Daimler Chrysler	(4.50)	44

Table 3 Toyota Sales & Market Cap Rank
(Source: finance.yahoo.com, annual reports)

Tables 3 through 6 compare units sold and market capitalization historically between the top selling automobile manufacturers. While some have gained in the units race by buying competitors, the charts readily show that Toyota continues to run away from their competitors today financially.

2008	Revenue	Loss	Units Sold	Cash	Debt	Market Value (2/09)
Toyota	265 B	-(4.5) B	9.24 M	52 B	131 B	102.7 B
GM	149 B	-(30.9) B	8.28 M	14 B	82 B	1.6 B
Ford	146 B	-(14.6) B	5.41 M	13.4 B	157 B	4.8 B

Table 4 2008 Great Recession Comparison
(Source: OICA and various news reports)

2001 (M)		2007 (M)		2010 (M)		2012 (M)		2015 (M)		2016 (M)	
GM	8.3	GM	9.4	Toyota	8.6	Toyota	10.1	Toyota	10.1	VW	10.31
Ford	6.9	Toyota	9.4	GM	8.5	GM	9.3	VW	10.0	Toyota	10.18
Toyota	5.9	Ford	6.6	VW	7.3	VW	9.3	GM	9.8	GM	9.97
VW	5.1	VW	6.2	Hyu-Kia	5.8	Hyu-Kia	7.1	Ren-Nis	8.5	Ren-Nis	9.96
Nissan	5.0	Honda	3.7	Ford	5.0	Ford	5.6	Hyu-Kia	7.9	Hyu-Kia	7.88

Table 5 Rank by Sold Units (Source: Statista)

	Apr 2002	Sep 2008	Aug 2011	Sep 2013	May 2016	Aug 2017
Toyota	101	140	112.3	206.3	152.1	186.3
VW	—	—	76.1	110.9	68.3	76.8
Ford	27	10	40	69.6	53.6	43.3
GM	34	6	34	51.5	48.3	51.6

Table 6 Market Cap in Billions (Source: YCharts)

Researchers at MIT found that TPS was so much more effective and efficient than traditional mass production that it represented a completely new paradigm and in *The Machine that Changed the World* they coined the term "Lean production" to indicate this radically different system for running a business.

WIREMOLD AND LANTECH

The Wiremold Company and Lantech LLC. were two private companies who began their Lean journey in the early 1990's. Their Lean stories are included in the book, *Lean Thinking*. Wiremold and Lantech both implemented Lean principles throughout the enterprise and were led in part by their CFO's, Orest Fiume and myself, respectively. After being encouraged by a Lean Manufacturing consultancy we both used, we chronicled our experience and gains made in applying Lean principles beyond manufacturing and creating Lean Accounting in our book, *Real Numbers.*

Wiremold[13] produces wire management systems and power and data protection products. It has facilities in the U.S., Europe, and the Far East. Led by their CEO, Art Byrne, Wiremold started a highly focused Lean effort in the early 1990s. After five years, their product-to-market development cycle was reduced by 75%. They had 16-18 new products per year versus 2-3 earlier. This with no headcount increases in the engineering or design team. Orders shipped in 20% of the time. The number of past due orders were down 90%. Order entry errors were nearly zero. Space required per given product volume was down 50% and productivity was increasing by 20% per year. Inventory turns went from 3.4 to 18.0. Wiremold began its Lean journey valued at $30 million and skyrocketed to a value of $770 million within 10 years.

Lantech makes packaging machinery including stretch wrapping machines and palletizers and has operations in both the U.S. and Europe. Like Wiremold and led by their CEO, Pat Lancaster, Lantech started a highly focused Lean effort in the early 1990s. In less than five years, Lantech was shipping twice as many machines with the same workforce of 300. 30% of their floor space was unused even though that same square footage was not enough in 1991. Defects per machine fell by a factor 10. Production throughput fell from 16 weeks to 14 hours. Weeks to hours! The ship date was met 90% of the time vs. 20% of the time in 1991.

It is important to understand when considering the gains at Wiremold and Lantech that both companies were market

THE VALUE ADD ACCOUNTANT

leaders in their respective industries before going Lean. These were already very good, well-run companies, and Lean still produced sensational gains allowing both of them to extend their leads over their competitors.

QUESTIONS FROM THE DOUBTING LEAN

There are a few questions that Lean practitioners—both new adopters and seasoned veterans—receive over and over from people who have not yet truly experienced the transformational power of Lean thinking. The questions are from colleagues concerning whether or not your Lean efforts are an effective, high value use of company time and resources.

"What is the value of Lean?" or some variant is the most asked Lean question overall. It's asked by everyone from the Chairman of the Board to the third shift maintenance worker. The word "value" can mean a thousand different things depending on who is doing the asking.

When someone participates in their first kaizen event, the questions often melt away since participants see the elimination of waste first hand. Best case—and it happens a lot—is when this change is a direct result of seeing something they revealed or suggested improving the process. Voila!

THE ACCOUNTING QUESTION

"What is the financial return of this kaizen event?"

That's it, by far the most common accounting-related question asked about Lean.

If your CFO or an accountant asks this or related questions, they are doing what they should be doing. They're verifying that company resources are being utilized in value adding ways.

The key word in the question is "financial." The answer

to this question immediately after any kaizen event is easy but not satisfying. "Immeasurable." Or, maybe "Zero." Or, maybe "Negative zero." As you probably already know or would guess, that answer does not play well to those who do not yet understand Lean transformation or the significant and ongoing value it delivers.

But, do not be confused. That does not mean the kaizen event did not have value. There is a difference between financial return and value. A well-executed kaizen event has very real, sustainable value. But the value begins with implementation of the process changes pulled out of the kaizen future state and compound thereafter each time the process is performed. Less waste, more available capacity, safer work environment, etc. forever and ever.

I have seen the strength of kaizen improvement events over and over and believe they are the single most important Lean tool to launch and sustain a Lean transformation. By no means the only tool; just the most important.

It is your job as a Lean thinker to provide a response that convinces the inquirer that value is being added even if it cannot be seen directly on a traditional financial report.

SUMMARY

As non-automotive manufacturers studied Toyota, they started using Toyota's waste reduction tools and building Toyota Production System principles into their own production strategic plans. They came to understand these concepts were universal in production environments, and TPS became known as "Lean Manufacturing" throughout the world.

Some thought leaders began thinking of Lean principles as universal and applicable to all business processes. As Lean application moved out of production into the business processes of manufacturing companies, it became clear that the Lean application could apply to service industries, hospitals, and many others. Today, every business segment has active Lean adherents. Even the U.S. military is a strong proponent of Lean thinking with many military branches being awarded the Shingo prize[14].

Here is a partial list—from my observations—of industries that are very active today with their adoption and promotion of Lean principles and tools.

- Automotive manufacturers and suppliers

- All types of discreet and process manufacturers

- Banking industry

- Healthcare industry

- Service
  - » Insurance
  - » Professional services
  - » Transportation
  - » Logistics

- Construction

- Government

- Military

- Retail

Where are the next horizons?

- Film industry

- Legal profession

- Agriculture

So, one strong argument for your CEO and CFO might be, "Your peers are doing this, why would you not?" Even with a desire to adopt Lean, few executives will go out on a limb with something new, until they can learn and see for themselves. Luckily, there are many, many resources now available to learn about Lean and to hear other stories.

Methods to learn:

- Conferences, seminars, & webinars

- Go to Gemba

- Fully participate in Lean improvement events

- Lean Books

- Contact a Lean-related consultant

- Chamber of Commerce and Trade associations

- Lean-related magazine articles

- Online training videos

- Peer-to-Peer discussion

- Manufacturing Extension Partnerships (MEPs)

Isolated learning may not do the trick either. Because as described in this book, many of the benefits require more than functional spend-reduction thinking to be fully actualized. The newly available capacity of people's time from eliminating wasteful activity will not leap directly to the income statement.

Use of the profit model, trends, and engaging your workers in new ways will be necessary to help the benefits be more obvious.

The Value Add Accountant must ensure that during the initial Lean efforts, executive knowledge and appreciation of Lean grows concurrently for they are absolutely critical for your company's sustained, long-term adoption of Lean thinking.

CONCLUSION

Throughout this book, a new role for the accounting/finance professional has been discussed. A role moving away from standard cost and transactional processing; moving away from bean counting; moving away from policing. This new role would instead move toward being part of value creation in the organization. This final chapter shares my view of what represents a value creating accountant and analyst.

Value Add Accountants want to know their business. Walking the process and observing the key steps is an important investigation. As a result, they understand the overall challenges of the process and where the process defect possibilities are high. They know the upstream and downstream processes of their work. An effort is put forth to know the people who do the work upstream and downstream.

The Value Add Accountant has a standard work day. It includes regular activities done hourly, daily, weekly, monthly and annually. Every task is performed consistently according to the standards. Standard work is used for areas where it is needed.

The Value Add Accountant is willing to teach their work to others understanding the value of adding organizational flexibility.

The Value Add Accountant has a visual office making it easy to see the sequence of work as well as what work is awaiting their attention. If a day off is needed, it is easier for a teammate to assist with their needed work based on the workplace organization. standard work, and cross-training.

The Value Add Accountant is willing to learn the job of other team members as needed so those team members can participate in kaizen events and strategic initiatives. Likewise, the Value Add Accountant participates in kaizen events and strategic initiatives.

The Value Add Accountant understands the purpose of the company and the current goals and objectives. They understand how their work contributes to achieving those targets and can discuss them with others.

The Value Add Accountant contributes at the daily huddle by sharing improvement ideas and volunteering to work on improvement activities. Ideas are put forth on how to improve their work. In addition to looking for waste and flow opportunities, they are willing to experiment in order to incorporate pace improvements and higher quality.

The Value Add Accountant is familiar with the computer systems that support the programs used in their direct functions as well as those used throughout the processes that they support. Partnering with a systems analyst, they periodically examine system features with an eye towards eliminating or avoiding existing manual, mind-numbing non-value add tasks. They also have the ability to use the system's report writer to create reports for their internal customers as well as to look for areas of defect that can be eliminated.

The Value Add Accountant values people, values curiosity, values innovation, and values experimentation. The Value Add Accountant is found outside the functional boundaries of accounting regularly.

And, the Value Add Accountant is thinking about the future.

GROUP THINK IS NEEDED!

Even in companies that have done a significant amount of Lean waste elimination activities, I still see evidence of well-meaning "improvers" sliding back into their traditional way of coming up with improvements on their own in a vacuum.

While individual improvements to one's immediate job are always encouraged, the desire to improve an overall process in a vacuum usually results in minimal gain at best and additional waste in many cases.

Individuals who think they know precisely how some other people should be doing their job are almost always mistaken.

So, take the time to plan and execute group-based Lean improvement events. Only a group that includes those actually doing the work brings the true current reality. That "reality" brainstorming improvements brings forth great accuracy and dramatic waste reduction in a process.

Avoid digressing back to improvements in a vacuum.

LEAN THINKING

As I am sure you have been able to tell in this book, I am a huge proponent of the concepts of Lean thinking. Lean thinking is the use of a set of principles and tools to identify unseen waste and eliminate it. It involves thinking, analysis, and experimentation. It does not adhere to a rule set or unbendable decrees.

I was at a networking session recently in Chicago. Trying

to describe what I do to people, who don't know what Lean or the Toyota Production System, is often mental fog time for the listener, and that is before I weigh in on Lean Accounting! But, that night I got a spark from one man who had heard of Lean Accounting. (Sort of a revelation in itself in a general crowd!)

He told me that Lean Accounting would not work in his industry. I couldn't let that go, so I asked him what industry? "Financial Services." So, I asked what there was in Lean Accounting that would not work there? From prior discussions rooted in this thought, I was expecting him to say that they don't manufacture, don't have inventory, or something like that. But instead he said that they have to "retain documentation."

I asked him what there was about Lean Accounting that would prevent the retention of documentation. Apparently, he had understood or been told, that one of the key elements of Lean Accounting is that you have to dispose of documents. I'm guessing that was from someone that defined all "documentation" as waste, meaning you had to get rid of all documentation. There is no Lean thinking in that idea. A process improvement event might well identify documentation within the process that can be eliminated, or digitized, or retained for regulatory purposes, or all of the above.

In the end, I assured him there is nothing in Lean Accounting, or any part of Lean, or the Toyota Production System that insists that there is any required work—documentation in this case—that should not be done because of some existing Lean tenet. A documentation trail would not be arbitrarily eliminated by a Lean method if it is required by a company or an industry (even if the customer doesn't care about it). Lean practitioners might try to reduce the time and costs surrounding the documentation, but any regulatory requirements have to be met or the business will suffer.

Now, what about you? Whether or not your company embraces Lean per se, you can still use Lean thinking, Lean concepts, and Lean tools to eliminate non-value add work in your office and drive towards the Value add accountant role discussed in this book. Rarely does anyone object to eliminating waste.

Is there something about Lean concepts or methodology that you feel would not be appropriate for your business? Before you use that thinking as a barrier to utilizing Lean thinking, I would be interested in hearing from you via email or otherwise. If you can be specific, that would be great, and we could have an interesting discussion.

THE PURPOSE OF ACCOUNTING
On the first day of the 7th annual Lean Accounting Summit[15], Dr. James Womack, the keynote speaker on the first day, asked us a fundamental question....

"What is the purpose of accounting?"

Immediately, an answer popped into my mind: "To see how the organization's experiments are doing!" Wow! I realized how truly far I had moved away from my former CFO role and into the world of Lean Thinking. That answer stayed with me throughout the conference.

For the last session, when everyone was getting overloaded with information, ideas, and actions to take, I listened to a presentation on system design by Dr. David S. Cochran. I almost didn't attend because I thought it might be too theoretical, and how would that fit with the more behavioral, practical perspective that I try to promote.

I was still thinking about accounting's role in helping everyone in the organization to see how the experiments are working. Dr. Cochran started out with this math looking equation. I was skeptical, but as he quietly explained it, I realized he was exactly in alignment with and illustrating my idea of accounting and experimentation.

The work done in every single process is an experiment unto itself. Taking Dr. Cochran's system design into my Lean Accounting world, his presentation revealed how the grand experiment—the company purpose—is a result of all the single, interrelated processes layered together. A company must know if those processes are moving the company efficiently towards its goals. In other words, is this approach, this grand experiment, working?

I often show clients how to use both outcome metrics and process metrics. Outcome metrics are used all the time by traditional companies and are very common. Process metrics are added by Lean companies, so they can communicate with employees about what is important to cause the process to continually improve. The idea is that when an improvement is implemented, the process metric can be tracked going forward to see if the improvement is having an impact on the process. With enough improvements and over time, the impact on financial outcome metrics will be seen as well.

So, if communicating how the organization's experiments are doing is the purpose of accounting, then accountants must understand the purpose of the experiments. Towards that end, what is accounting trying to learn? What is accounting trying to get better at? When accounting understands the separate experiments, then they can provide the information that would most effectively reflect the performance of the companywide grand experiment.

I walked away from the Lean Accounting Summit once

again reminded that there is much to learn about these Lean Accounting and wider Lean Office matters. Luckily, today there are lots of books, workshops, conferences, and, hopefully, your own internal improvement events to do just that.

And as each of us learns, we need to always be thinking about how we can best use what we are learning. We need to continue the experiments.

We need to take action.

ENDNOTES

1   Ryan Davies and Douglas Huey (April 2017). *Why CFOs Need A Bigger Role in Business Transformations.* McKinsey Special Collection: The Role of the CFO.

2   Jeremy Hope (2009). The CFO as Analyst and Adviser. Excerpted from *Reinventing the CFO: How Financial Managers Can Transform Their Roles and Add Greater Value* (Harvard Business Press)

3   James P. Womack, Daniel T. Jones, and Daniel Roos, *The Machine That Changed the World* (New York: Scribner, 1990)

4   James P. Womack and Daniel T. Jones, *Lean Thinking: Banish Waste and Create Wealth in Your Corporation* (New York: Simon & Schuster, 1996)

5   Jean E. Cunningham and Orest J. Fiume, *Real Numbers: Management Accounting in a Lean Organization* (Jean Cunningham Consulting, 2003)

6   Jean Cunningham and Duane Jones, *Easier, Simpler, Faster: Systems Strategy for Lean IT* (Productivity Press, 2007)

7   Jean E. Cunningham and Orest J. Fiume, *Real Numbers: Management Accounting in a Lean Organization* (Jean Cunningham Consulting, 2003)

8   The Association for Manufacturing Excellence. Created in 1985, AME is manufacturing centric, but includes the entire universe of continuous improvement tools and methods.

9   MEP stands for "Manufacturing Extension Partnership." MEPs were created by the Commerce Department in all 50 states to help coordinate improvements in small manufacturers. Many MEPs have become clearing houses for continuous improvement information including seminars, webinars, and site visits.

10   Lean Enterprise Institute. LEI was started by Jim Womack in 1997 and is a global force of Lean education. LEI conducts research, teaches educational workshops, publishes books and eBooks, runs conferences, and shares practical information about Lean thinking and practice.

11   Art Byrne, The Lean Turnaround, How Business Leaders Use Lean Principles to Create Value and Transform Their Company (McGraw-Hill, 2013)

12   Jacob Stoller, The Lean CEO, Leading the Way to World-Class Excellence (McGraw- Hill Education, 2015)

13   Wiremold Company was bought by Legrand S. A. in 2000 soon after Wiremold's Lean renaissance.

14   Awarded by the Shingo Institute annually to publications that advance operational excellence and to organizations that have shown commitment to operational excellence.

15   The annual Lean Accounting Summit is managed by Lean Frontiers. First held in 2005, it was the premier conference focused on Lean Accounting. It remains the leading gathering of Lean Accounting expertise and the best concentrated learning opportunity available.

INDEX

CPSIA information can be obtained
at www.ICGtesting.com
Printed in the USA
LVHW04s2158160618
580548LV00001B/1/P